Good Enough Parenting is overflowing with practical, evidence-based, nonprescriptive strategies for how to raise children through tough times with confidence, hope, and self-compassion. As a school counselor who works with parents who often fear they're not "enough," I appreciate that the authors, psychologists Tim Cavell and Lauren Quetsch, approach the topic with warmth, wisdom, and frequent reminders that love is caregivers' greatest superpower.

—PHYLLIS L. FAGELL, LCPC, SCHOOL COUNSELOR, PSYCHOTHERAPIST, JOURNALIST, AND AUTHOR OF *MIDDLE SCHOOL MATTERS*

Cavell and Quetsch do a masterful job of giving parents a holistic, effective approach to raising children. They zoom out on parenting, describing the context that makes it so difficult, then give readers a practical plan, filled with quick, easy-to-execute exercises to orient parents towards being "good enough." A must-read for new and seasoned parents alike!

—REGINE GALANTI, PhD, DIRECTOR OF LONG ISLAND BEHAVIORAL PSYCHOLOGY, AND AUTHOR OF *ANXIETY RELIEF FOR TEENS* AND *WHEN HARLEY HAS ANXIETY*

Finally, a book that recognizes that parents aren't and can't be perfect! *Good Enough Parenting* offers science-based, realistic guidance on what matters most—building a positive and effective parent–child relationship.

—MARY K. ALVORD, PhD, PSYCHOLOGIST AND COAUTHOR OF *CONQUER NEGATIVE THINKING FOR TEENS* AND *RESILIENCE BUILDER PROGRAM FOR CHILDREN AND ADOLESCENTS*

T0035910

As practical as it is deeply thought provoking, *Good Enough Parenting* teaches the science of good parenting, using easily understandable language and a validating tone. Drs. Cavell and Quetsch explain how to mindfully assess and adjust one's parenting as children grow, making the book as useful to parents of toddlers as it is to parents of teens.

—DANIELA J. OWEN, PhD, CLINICAL PSYCHOLOGIST AND
AUTHOR OF *RIGHT NOW, I AM FINE* AND
EVERYONE FEELS ANGRY SOMETIMES SERIES

Parenting is the hardest work there is! This book offers comprehensive, evidence-based guidance in an encouraging and practical way. Parents may struggle with different things, but all will find something helpful here.

—MARY ANN McCABE, PhD, ABPP, ASSOCIATE CLINICAL PROFESSOR
OF PEDIATRICS, GEORGE WASHINGTON UNIVERSITY SCHOOL
OF MEDICINE AND HEALTH SCIENCES, WASHINGTON, DC

The single most important decision an adult can make is to become a parent. Parenting is a lifelong commitment that is guaranteed to be challenging and exhausting quite often, but with *Good Enough Parenting* skills, it is the most treasured and fulfilling role that life has to offer. Cavell and Quetsch provide parents with the guidebook we've all been waiting for! These experts offer a clear, step-by-step, evidence-based approach to guiding children toward prosocial and emotionally healthy attitudes, as well as the skills and behaviors that will propel them into young adulthood. Most important, the authors help parents accept and embrace the idea that taking care of themselves will lead to more loving and effective parenting of their kids. Well done!

—ANNE MARIE ALBANO, PhD, ABPP, CLINICAL PSYCHOLOGIST AND
FOUNDING DIRECTOR, COLUMBIA UNIVERSITY CLINIC FOR ANXIETY
AND RELATED DISORDERS, NEW YORK, NY

This book is packed with science-based, practical strategies for parents of children of all ages. The authors advise with profound respect for parents and the hard work of parenting. They offer real-life examples and exercises parents can use right away. Their approach is hopeful and will be especially valuable for parents who are experiencing parenting challenges. I highly recommend this book.

—**ELLEN R. DeVOE, PhD, LICSW,** PROFESSOR AND ASSOCIATE DEAN, BOSTON UNIVERSITY SCHOOL OF SOCIAL WORK, BOSTON, MA

Good Enough Parenting embraces the vital concept that effective parenting is not a set of disconnected techniques that you apply uniformly to every child. Rather, it is about maximizing your relationship with the child you have and being the responsive parent that they need. Cavell and Quetsch capture this concept beautifully by offering practical concepts that leverage the science of effective youth interventions to benefit any parent looking to build a more positive relationship with their child.

—**JILL EHRENREICH-MAY, PhD,** PROFESSOR, UNIVERSITY OF MIAMI, CORAL GABLES, FL, AND AUTHOR OF *UNIFIED PROTOCOLS FOR TRANSDIAGNOSTIC TREATMENT OF EMOTIONAL DISORDERS IN CHILDREN AND ADOLESCENTS*

Every parent or caregiver will see themselves and their children in the stories that come alive in the pages of this book. I highly recommend it if you are seeking practical, straightforward, culturally competent child-rearing guidance based on psychological science.

—**TERRY STANCIN, PhD, ABPP,** PROFESSOR OF PEDIATRICS, PSYCHIATRY, PHYSICAL MEDICINE & REHABILITATION, AND PSYCHOLOGICAL SCIENCES, CASE WESTERN RESERVE UNIVERSITY, CLEVELAND, OH

What a relief! In an age of so-much, too-much information *Good Enough Parenting* is a book that fills the mental gap between being and doing. Expert navigation of the science is provided by Cavell and Quetsch's Six-Point Plan, but the nuggets of the authors' own personal experiences, sprinkled throughout, are the real gold. Self-doubting parents can truly understand good enough parenting, by learning how the experts reconcile their own education and science with their parenting experiences.

—CLARISSA ESCOBAR-AGUILAR, PhD, CLINICAL PSYCHOLOGIST IN PRIMARY CARE, DIRECTOR OF PSYCHOLOGY/TRAINING AT THE CENTER FOR HEALTH CARE SERVICES; ASSISTANT PROFESSOR, DEPARTMENT OF FAMILY AND COMMUNITY MEDICINE AND DEPARTMENT OF PSYCHIATRY AT UT-HEALTH SAN ANTONIO, SAN ANTONIO, TX

GOOD ENOUGH
Parenting

TIMOTHY A. CAVELL, *PhD*
LAUREN B. QUETSCH, *PhD*

GOOD ENOUGH
Parenting

A SIX-POINT PLAN *for*
a STRONGER RELATIONSHIP
WITH YOUR CHILD

 AMERICAN PSYCHOLOGICAL ASSOCIATION

Published by
APA LifeTools
750 First Street, NE
Washington, DC 20002
https://www.apa.org

Order Department
https://www.apa.org/pubs/books
order@apa.org

In the U.K., Europe, Africa, and the Middle East, copies may be ordered from Eurospan
https://www.eurospanbookstore.com/apa
info@eurospangroup.com

Typeset in Sabon by Circle Graphics, Inc., Reisterstown, MD

Printer: Sheridan Books, Chelsea, MI
Cover Designer: Mark Karis

Library of Congress Cataloging-in-Publication Data

Names: Cavell, Timothy A., author. | Quetsch, Lauren B., author.
Title: Good enough parenting : a six-point plan for a stronger relationship
   with your child / by Timothy A. Cavell and Lauren B. Quetsch.
Description: Washington, DC : American Psychological Association, [2022] |
   Includes bibliographical references and index.
Identifiers: LCCN 2022020490 (print) | LCCN 2022020491 (ebook) | ISBN
   9781433839115 (paperback) | ISBN 9781433839122 (ebook)
Subjects: LCSH: Parenting--Psychological aspects. | Parent and
   child--Psychological aspects. | Child psychology. | BISAC: FAMILY &
   RELATIONSHIPS / Parenting / General | PSYCHOLOGY / Developmental /
   Child
Classification: LCC BF723.P25 C38 2023 (print) | LCC BF723.P25 (ebook) |
   DDC 155.4--dc23/eng/20220716
LC record available at https://lccn.loc.gov/2022020490
LC ebook record available at https://lccn.loc.gov/2022020491

https://doi.org/10.1037/0000324-000

Printed in the United States of America

10 9 8 7 6 5 4 3 2

The workshop of character is everyday life.
—Maltbie D. Babcock

The joys of parents are secret, and so are their grieves and fears.
—Francis Bacon

CONTENTS

PREFACE

At its core, parenting is a relationship—the relationship you have with your children over time. Some of the most important questions in life are answered by the relationship children have with their parents. Am I loved? Do I matter? Am I safe? How should I treat others? Are there things I shouldn't do? Who will hold me accountable? Whose example will I follow? Your job as parents is to manage that relationship, often for the rest of your lives. Our job is to help you do that.

We are child/family psychologists trained to know the risks that signal concern about a child's development. We are also scholars who study evidence-based parenting interventions. Our training and expertise are handy tools, but none of that matters if we fail to treat parents with the respect they deserve or the understanding they need. Our hope is that you see how important you are to your child, regardless of past doubts or previous missteps. We also hope you see in yourself the potential we see in all parents. And we hope you come to know that your own health and well-being are precious gifts to your children.

This is a book for those who are curious about what matters most in parenting. More specifically, it's a book for parents who want to see their children grow to become adults who manage their emotions, control their behavior, and enjoy their relationships. Our aim is to offer workable, science-informed guidance based on the notion that parenting is first and foremost a relationship. Your relationship with your child is unique, with an emotional past and a hoped-for future; it also happens to be your best tool as a parent.

We aspire to honor the science of child development by adopting a holistic approach to good enough parenting. We see parenting as more than a loose collection of short-term fixes cut apart from the life course of the parent–child relationship. We don't want you feeling criticized or confused by our guidance. Parents can read lots of books and magazines, listen to experts, talk with family and friends, and still be unsure. We hope to offer advice that is sensible and doesn't condemn. We want you to feel confident about where to put your time and energy and let go of standards that require perfect parenting. We want you to focus on what matters most.

FROM LAUREN

When I was a new, starry-eyed graduate student, a mother came to our training clinic with her 4-year-old son. He played on the floor quietly, uncertain about this new environment—moving the toys slowly and carefully across the floor. As we discussed the mother's concerns and why she came to the clinic, she looked at me, leaned in close, and whispered just loud enough so I could hear but her son could not, "I love my child, but . . . I don't like my child." That one statement by a mother desperate for hope stuck in my brain in a way I was not expecting. I understood it at a surface level when I first heard it, but it was many years later before I finally understood what she was trying to communicate.

The mother's comment speaks to what many parents feel but have difficulty expressing: "I love my child, but I don't always like my child." It's that combination of unwavering, unmovable love for your child accompanied at times by feeling frustrated or bewildered, feelings that cause parents to wonder, "How long will this last?" and "Is this normal?" If these feelings persist, they lead to self-doubt and fears about being a bad parent. As many have learned, the job of parenting can change as children grow, but the challenges are not necessarily easier. A parent's job unfolds and shifts over time: Concerns about sleep soon become worries about tantrums, which later morph into toileting issues, and then shapeshift into anxieties about sharing, being liked by peers, finding success at school, or lying to adults . . . you get the idea. Many of these concerns are natural and expected when we're caring for and setting limits on little humans whose job is to discover the world around them. But if parents dread spending time with their child, when they feel emotionally and physically drained by the job of parenting, or when they believe that they "must be the worst parent in the world," well, then, it might be time to recalibrate.

I welcome you to this book with the hope that we can help unwind any confusion you feel as a parent and create greater confidence as you embrace this fulfilling but challenging role. I'm a clinical psychologist with a specialization in parenting young children. But I'm also a mother of four young children. No matter who you are, parenting can be a daunting task. We hope you approach this book not to figure out "who parents best" or whether you are "doing it correctly" but as a way to find what works best for you and your family. Parent–child relationships are not simple, off-the-rack kinds of things. Each is custom-made, and our aim is to ensure a comfortable, well-tailored "fit."

This book recognizes the complexity of parenting. Ideally, we'll help you recognize your strengths, build on your values, and allow you to feel more at peace with the decisions you make as the head of your family. If you're reading this, you've already taken a big step. As you move through the book, we encourage you to recognize and accept two truths: You can love your child *and* you can find it hard to like your child. There is no benefit to ignoring the emotional expense that comes with parenting. It's better to see it and to have a workable plan for the tough times ahead. Our hope is that you'll see your love for your child as a superpower, one you can access even when you're confused, angry, or broken. Read this book, lead with love, and learn what matters most in being not a perfect parent but one that is good enough.

FROM TIM

As a therapist, I often work with parents who ask for guidance about their children. I listen to their concerns, and I try to help. I learn about a boy who is sullen and angry, hits his sisters, defies his mom, and says he hates everyone and everything. But I also learn that his mom loves him and is filled with worry about his future. I meet the parents of a middle school girl who cries in bed at night because she wishes she had "just one good friend," someone she felt close to. Her parents cry too, wishing her dream would come true. I listen as parents talk about their talented teenage son who hasn't been home in 3 days. Some families are all too familiar with the rhythm of disorder. When the stories are messy and when parents ache with regret, seethe with anger, or break with sadness, I feel weighed down. I believe I can help parents weather the storms of child-rearing, and I think about these families a lot. Sometimes I have my own doubts about my ability to help—I see my limits.

However, my research and training give me the confidence I need to be an effective family therapist. Even still, there are no guarantees. The same is true for parenting. My wife and I have three children—all are now young adults living on their own. I'd like to believe our parenting mattered and that we made a positive difference in their lives. But there were certainly times when our ability to protect and guide them was limited, when our influence could go only so far. There were also times when we made a real mess of parenting. We'd get mad and blow up, make unreasonable demands, or give in too easily. And yet, despite our limits, we did a lot right. With each child, we tried to have the kind of relationship that invited them to invest in and follow our example. We are grateful that we can celebrate the gift of our three children and their healthy adult lives. Of course, much of that could change tomorrow unexpectedly. So, today we celebrate that we aren't the worst parents in the world. But we sure know that feeling.

Here's what I hope this book can offer. The first is a way to make sense of the "worst-parent-in-the-world" feeling. It's actually pretty common. I mention it to parents and never have to explain it. Less well known are the reasons—science-based reasons—why some feel like the worst parent in the world. The second thing is a position from which to parent. *Position* is a useful word for parents because few things are as important as the *place* we hold in our family, the *perspective* we have about the job of parenting, and the *posture* we take when interacting with our children. The goal of this book is to help you develop a long-term, workable plan for good enough parenting—one that's a good fit for you and your family, something that will last. Ideally, what we offer is practical and useful. It won't make you a perfect parent or give you perfect children, but you'll be parenting from a place of hope, where your actions toward your children are generally healthy, wise, caring, competent, and, well, good enough.

GOOD ENOUGH
Parenting

INTRODUCTION

WHY READ THIS BOOK?

From the first moment you see, touch, and (yes) smell your newborn child, a relationship is formed—a relationship that can bring countless moments of joy, love, and pride as well as bouts of frustration, sadness, and fear. As author Elizabeth Stone wrote, being a parent "is to decide forever to have your heart go walking outside your body." The bond you have with your child is unique among all your life's relationships. When the parent–child relationship is managed well, it is a powerful resource for children. It helps them grow, learn, and make their way through life. But what does it mean to "manage well" the parent–child relationship?

Perhaps you're reading this book because your relationship with your child is not quite what it should be or what you had imagined. Perhaps you see your *children* as not quite who they should be or what you had imagined. Perhaps you're a parent who worries about your children's future or their recent past. Or perhaps you're simply a parent who wonders, "Am I doing this right?" We assume you're reading this book because you're invested in the work of parenting and want what's best for your children.

This book is meant to *be* two things. First, this book can be a stand-alone guide for parents concerned about parenting or concerned about a child aged 18 years or under who is having emotional or behavior problems. But it's also a companion to another book we wrote specifically for *therapists* who work with parents whose children are defiant and aggressive (Cavell & Quetsch, 2023). By design, the contents of this book and the therapist book overlap substantially, which should help parents working with a therapist on child- and family-related problems. Hopefully, therapists will use the overlapping content to work collaboratively with parents. We also hope parents will use this book to stay fully informed when seeking the help of a professional therapist.

This book is also meant to *do* two things. First, it will help you gauge those aspects of parenting that are going well and those that might need work. We don't present a long list of parenting skills that invites you to feel lacking or inept; instead, we offer a plan for what matters most in parenting. If your goal is to be a parent good enough to meet your children's needs—not a perfect parent—then this is the book for you. Second, this book will help you build a workable plan for parenting. You'll learn about six major areas of parenting and how to use that information to make a plan that fits your family.

WHY IS PARENTING OFTEN DIFFICULT OR CONFUSING?

There are several reasons why parenting is often difficult or confusing. Here are three of them.

Reason 1: Parenting Is One-Sided

For the most part, parenting is a one-sided gig: Children depend on us for lots of things, for a long time. Willard Hartup, a well-known developmental psychologist, described children's relationships with parents as *vertical attachments*. They are vertical in the sense that parents have greater knowledge and social power than children do.

As babies, our children are entirely dependent on us, both physically and emotionally. As they get older, they become more independent but still need us, only in different ways. With time, children begin to spend less and less time with us, but we still carry that sense of responsibility and concern. Added to the work and the weight of parenting is the fact that you can't expect to get out of parenting as much as you put into it. Yes, having children can greatly enrich our lives and give special meaning to our existence, but parents generally give to children more than they get in return. That's how nature arranged it, and it is certainly true today now that children are less often viewed as essential personnel for the family farm or the family business. But it is also true in terms of the emotional rewards we hope to get from parenting—that sense of love, understanding, and connection we imagine is an essential by-product of parenting. Indeed, there are times when the payoff for parenting seems unfair and one-sided. This book can help you adjust to that likelihood so you won't miss the special, heart-warming, teary-eyed moments that are also a part of child-rearing.

Reason 2: Parents Have Limited Control Over Their Children's Behavior

A second reason why parenting can be difficult or confusing is that *we have limited control over our children's behavior.* Parents play an important role in child development, but even the most effective parents are not puppeteers, able to make children perform however and whenever they choose. In fact, any guilt you feel as a parent could stem from specialists like us putting too much emphasis on how parenting influences children's growth and development. Consider the old saying, "As the twig is bent, so grows the tree," which is often interpreted to mean that good parents raise good kids and bad parents raise bad kids. Today, science tells a different story about the role of parental influence, even though public opinion still has us judging and often condemning parents whose children are behaving "badly." If you're the parent of a child who is overly active, strong-willed, or has trouble learning in the usual way, you know what we mean. Some children will cause *any* parent to struggle.

A more up-to-date story about parenting and child development has several parts. The first is that genes matter a great deal—not just in how children look (skin color, height) but also in their talents, abilities, and personality. Genetic endowment also shapes how children respond to and learn from their environment. For example, some infants have an easy temperament that allows them to fit into whatever schedule of feeding, changing, and sleeping parents prefer. Others have a more difficult temperament and are less predictable and less easily scheduled. Recent studies also show that many psychological disorders involve inherited vulnerabilities that when combined with significant life stress can lead to large problems down the road. In fact, it is fair to say that experts in human development no longer assume that parenting is more important or more influential than genetics. Instead, today's experts assume that both matter and recognize that both act on the other to influence children's development. A second part of the story about parenting and child development is that parents are just one source of environmental influence. Scientists now recognize that many other contexts affect children's development. Among these are their interactions with siblings, peers, grandparents, teachers, and coaches as well as their exposure to technology and various sources of media. Scholars such as Judith Rich Harris have argued that parents actually have *less* influence than other external factors (e.g., peers, teachers) in children's lives! None of the newer research on nature versus nurture refutes the critical role parents play in children's lives, but it does help inform parents about what truly matters.

Reason 3: The Myth of Effective Parenting

A third reason why parenting can be difficult or confusing is what we call the *myth of effective parenting.* In today's information age, there is no shortage of advice for parents, but not all of it is helpful, and misplaced emphasis on effective parenting is one of the subtler ways parents can be made to feel like they're stumbling. This myth usually begins with a message that experts have identified a specific set of child-rearing skills that are recommended for all parents regardless of the parent, the child, or the circumstances affecting the family and the context for child-rearing (e.g., culture, divorce, alcoholism, poverty). Next is the implication that if children are behaving "badly," then parents must lack effective parenting skills. The last part of the myth is that effective parenting means using the "right" skill at the "right" time in the "right" way. If parents do this, there should be no reason to struggle and no reason for child misbehavior.

Like many myths, there are kernels of truth. It is true that research has pinpointed the kinds of parenting behavior that are linked with negative child outcomes. Big-ticket items include overly harsh or rejecting parenting; parenting that is lax and without restrictions; and parenting that is neglectful or is physically, emotionally, or sexually abusive. We also know that providing consistent discipline, fostering a sense of belonging, and monitoring children's whereabouts and activities outside the home positively predict children's adjustment. Where these findings become myth is when they are recast as a narrow list of prescribed parenting skills and presented as the definitive statement on how to parent. It's an approach that loses sight of the parent–child relationship. The myth of effective parenting also tends to emphasize the short-term management of children's misbehavior; less emphasis is placed on managing the parent–child relationship over time (i.e., for 18-plus years).

When parenting is framed this way, it can push parents to see the trees but not the forest. Parents whose children are struggling emotionally or behaviorally will feel like failures when problems persist or when the parent–child relationship is further strained. In this book, we take a different approach to parenting. Our goal is to offer a workable, long-term, science-based plan that parents can use to address a wide range of emotional and behavioral issues affecting children and families. We invite you to learn about the six-point plan for good enough parenting. We welcome you to learn about what matters most.

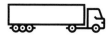

CHAPTER I

HOLISTIC, LONG-TERM PARENTING: FROM TODDLERS TO TEENS

Jason is on a work call with his boss when his 5-year-old son, Sean, swings the door open and walks in. Jason is annoyed that he forgot to lock the door and tries to wave Sean away, as he was hoping to use the call to make a good impression.

Sean says excitedly, "Dad! Who are you on the phone with? Is it Grandma? Can I tell her hi?"

Jason apologizes to his boss, turns toward his son, and mouths, "Get out of here."

Sean protests, "But, Dad, you promised I could hold the phone the next time we called Grandma."

Jason is frustrated and raises his voice. "Get out of the room, Sean! Now! I'm on a call!"

Sean is confused but leaves quickly, his eyes welling with tears.

After the call, Jason walks into the living room and finds Sean watching TV. Jason turns off the TV and shows his irritation with his son: "Sean! You know better than to walk in when my door is closed! I was on an important call! You never listen! You could have ruined the whole thing. Sometimes you are so selfish and disrespectful! And you're not supposed to be watching shows right now. Go to your room!"

Later, Jason tries to make sense of what happened and how he responded to his son.

How would you define the "job" of parenting? We assume most parents would say parents are supposed to protect, feed, clothe, and shelter their children. Others might add that parents make sure children attend school and care for them when they're sick. But what else goes with the job? Most would agree that a parent should teach important life lessons, such as the difference between right and wrong, how to get along with others, and what it takes to get ahead in this world. But is there a right and wrong way to do this teaching? Is it better to speak loudly or whisper gently? When is it time to preach and when is it time to punish? How do we know if we're being too strict or not strict enough? Is there a reliable way to know when parenting is going well?

In our experience, few parents spend time thinking about the downstream effects of parenting. Instead, parenting is done in the moment: We respond to sibling arguments, we ask about schoolwork, we fix dinner, we put our kids to bed, and we do it all over again the next day. But parenting is also an opportunity to make a long-term investment in our children's lives. By being present each day—physically and emotionally—we can provide valuable life lessons, an example to follow, and continuous affirmation and support. All of this can add up to our children becoming healthy, responsible, and emotionally stable adults, but it will require a healthy, safe, and supportive parent–child relationship. We do the job of parenting when we move in rhythm with our children—over time. This is the best kind of parenting.

This chapter aims to help you

- recognize how you tend to judge your parenting, and
- learn a more workable way to define *good parenting*.

AM I A GOOD ENOUGH PARENT?

You might have heard of the term *good enough parent*. The good enough parent is one who isn't trying to be perfect and doesn't expect perfection from their children. It's a useful concept to keep in mind, especially if you're someone who tends to make perfect the enemy of the good. With some exceptions, of course, there's plenty of room for parents to mess up and ample time to correct course. It's okay to be good enough, but it may be unclear what it means to be a good enough parent.

Let's look at various ways parents might evaluate their parenting. While some of these are helpful measuring sticks to get back on track, others can lead parents astray as they spend time and energy on things that don't really matter.

How My Child Acts

This is an obvious and widely used parenting benchmark: We gauge our parenting based on how and what our children are doing. If they are bringing home good report cards, doing their chores, and staying out of trouble, then we must be good enough parents, right? Perhaps, but developmental studies often indicate that children's traits and talents are linked more to their genetic endowment than to their childhood experiences. We can look pretty good as parents when our children are born with a strong proclivity to be cooperative and agreeable. But not all of us are so lucky; we didn't get the "mild-mannered" child. In fact, depending on their traits and talents, your children might pursue specific activities, make certain choices, and hang out with particular individuals. A 12-year-old boy who is 6-feet, 3-inches tall and naturally athletic could spend lots of time and energy engaged in sports, whereas a 9-year-old girl who has been playing piano since the age of 4 might gravitate toward musical pursuits. The bottom line here is that we can't claim sole responsibility when our children succeed *and* we shouldn't shoulder all the blame when things go badly.

Determining whether your child's behavior is a problem can also be complicated. Imagine your daughter eating nothing but bacon for breakfast. You offer cereal, eggs, and fruit and she only wants bacon. You tell her she can't have bacon—that she should try other foods—and she gets upset and throws a fit. At what point and by what criteria do you decide that bacon eating is a problem? When does it go from being "okay" to a thing that needs to be changed? And how do you decide if a behavior is something you should address or something you let your children learn for themselves? Some parents try to help their child avoid *every* risk or *any* failure. They are stuck in parenting overdrive hoping to "make sure" their child is not hurt or led astray. So, be cautious about using your child's behavior as the go-to benchmark when judging your parenting: You could be deceiving yourself when things are going well, and it could be defeating when things go poorly.

What Others Expect

Sometimes we use others' expectations to gauge our parenting successes and failures. If you're lucky, your friends and relatives will talk about what a great job you're doing. But you also might hear concerns or criticisms: "Does your son always cry like that?" "Are you sure it's just a phase your daughter's going through?" "Have you heard what people are saying about your daughter and her boyfriend?" Comments like this can really sting. Sometimes these concerns arrive as formal reports with significant consequences (e.g., removal from day care, bad grades, criminal charges), so it's important to consider whether there's any corrective action for you to take. But more often, others' expectations are not a useful way to gauge the quality of our parenting. Others are not in our shoes and not in our homes and families, so their judgments can hurt more than help.

What My Parents Did

This kind of measuring stick exists whether you want it or not. Few of us get formal training in how to be a parent, so what we learn is often taken from the pages of our childhood. But even if we believe our parents did a great job, it doesn't mean we fully understand what they did or why it "worked." There's also the problem of poor recall; it's easy to misremember how you were parented and successfully imitating your parents is no guarantee that it's right for your children. Parents like to say, "Well it worked for me!" without considering whether their children have the same temperament or tendencies they did. So, be careful about quickly adopting hand-me-down parenting strategies. This is especially true if it means perpetuating a history of poor parenting or possible child abuse.

Opposite of My Parents

When we believe our own parents made a mess of our childhood, a common goal is to never be our parents! We see a lot of this in our clinical practice. It's usually reported as a strong vow to parent in a way that is opposite of what their parents did. There are two key problems with this standard. First, it's not a great guide for what parents should do, and it's not entirely clear how parents should avoid the mistakes of their parents. For example, a parent might vow to never put their kids through a divorce, failing to recognize that their partner could, at some point, come to a different decision about their marriage. The second problem with this approach is that it's hard to avoid using words and actions you heard and saw daily as a child. We certainly admire parents who want to break from the pattern of poor parenting they received, but it can be hard to parent differently from what we experienced. Parents who promise to do this will likely need some guidance to make it happen.

How My Child Feels

Another way parents might gauge the quality of their parenting is by reading and responding to their children's emotions. It makes sense

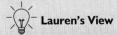

Lauren's View

Even if I give my screaming toddlers what they want, there are still times when they melt to the ground, seemingly crushed and confused by the weight of this cruel world I've created for them.

that children who are happy and content might have parents who are doing things right; conversely, children who are irritable and upset might have parents who are slipping up and parenting badly. Thus, it's tempting to make our parenting decisions based on our children's emotional reactions. What parent wouldn't want to put a smile on the face of a child who is on the ground screaming and crying?

Who enjoys seeing unhappy children when we punish their misbehavior? And yet, we know that protecting children from tough emotional experiences can rob them of the opportunity to learn how to manage their emotions. Consider the times when your children might be really scared, incredibly sad, or highly disappointed, such as when they find out that their grandmother has terminal cancer, that they didn't make the soccer team, or that it's scary to learn to ride a bike. Many of us are pulled to steer clear of these tough moments; we don't want our children to ache. But wise parenting decisions, ones that benefit our children, often involve discomfort and unpleasant feelings.

Please don't misunderstand: It is important to pay attention to our children's feelings, and when parents are emotionally unavailable or rejecting, it can harm children. But being in tune with children's feelings is *not* the same thing as trying to limit or manage what our children feel. When your son tells you that he sat alone at lunch because his best friends were not at school, you want to be tuned in to the emotions that came with this event. You want him to know you're listening and trying to understand. Your behavior sends a strong message that says, "It's safe to tell me what you're feeling." The goal is not to fix whatever led to his unpleasant feelings. If you need your children to be happy, or if you judge yourself harshly when they show tears or tantrums, you could be falling into a deceptive and dangerous pattern. It is better to be present and let your children feel their emotions—pleasant and unpleasant.

How I Feel

Parenthood can bring us into contact with utter joy as well as heart-wrenching sadness, but the fact that parents have all these feelings doesn't mean we should use them as our measuring stick. Emotions can sometimes distort or disrupt the way we parent. We've all done this to some degree. We feel joyful and festive, so we forget about the bedtime curfew or ignore the rule about no food in the living room. We feel tired and cranky, so we tighten our hold, strictly enforcing every rule and giving children little room to err. Or we might feel hopeless and discouraged, so we temporarily check out from the job of parenting, letting children fend for themselves or insisting they take care of us. And if we feel angry and attacked, we might lash out and hurt the younger members of our family.

There are times when our emotions are a by-product of what we see and feel in our children. When they're scared, we're scared. When they're sad, we're sad. Sometimes there's precious little distance between our children's discomfort and our own discomfort. So, if you're a parent who cares about your children and often feel what they feel, then you'll need a way to manage those feelings while still parenting wisely. Otherwise, you could be on the slippery slope of emotion-driven parenting. There's no need to ignore your emotions when parenting, but parents need an effective strategy for managing (and using) their emotions (see Chapter 3).

The Best I Can Do

Parents who feel lost and defeated sometimes arrive at this potentially problematic benchmark. Of course, it is, in some ways, a way for parents

15

to cope. But it can also be a type of surrender. As therapists, we believe parents are doing their best at any time, considering their circumstances and resources. Parents who feel hopeless and discouraged can find it hard to make even small gains. But if "the best I can do" means ignoring the possibility of change and growth, it can become a place to hide—a place that produces unhealthy habits that parents never intended.

We should note that it is not uncommon for parents to periodically change the criteria by which they judge their child-rearing. They might start trying to emulate their parents (or the opposite of their parents). But if their children begin to show signs of emotional distress or behavior problems, then they'll consider experts' advice on "effective parenting." If their concerns persist, they might then adjust their expectations to what makes them feel better. The most difficult place for parents to land is believing it's too late to help their children or change their parenting. It's easy to be discouraged when children repeatedly falter, when they move dangerously onto a life path that is unhealthy, risky, or illegal.

Our message to discouraged parents is to see and celebrate their parenting *efforts*—not their parenting outcomes. Parents' persistent efforts to support and guide their child are the surest sign of their love. Children's development can be influenced by so many variables—biogenetic factors, personality, talents, family resources, relationships with family and nonfamily members, strong interests, early achievements—but parents have limited control over many of these factors. What parents can control is being engaged and supportive, investing and reinvesting in their children's well-being. When working with discouraged parents, we generally deliver this message to both them and their children, especially if the children are teenagers:

> I've told your parents that the most loving thing they can do is to keep at it, keep trying to be the parent you need, even when they're getting it wrong and when you don't like it and don't want their

help. I have advised them to not give up on you. If you're lucky, they'll take my advice. You might not like it, but you'll still be lucky.

A WORKABLE PLAN FOR PARENTING

We believe parents are helped when they have a **simple, straightforward** plan for parenting. This plan should be **practical, sustainable, and supported by the science** of parenting and child development. Ideally, this plan promotes healthy child development while also valuing the health and well-being of the parent. It guides parents on when and where to focus their time and energy. It identifies those aspects of parenting that matter most. And it's sustainable over time, across the years of parenting. This book is our attempt to offer such a plan. In today's world, parents are busy and compete with many other influences for their children's time and attention. Our hope is that parents who read this book will have a workable plan going forward. Next, we present a **holistic, long-term model of parenting**. In the fields of health and medicine, the term *holistic* means focusing on the whole person and addressing broader social and emotional needs and not just the symptoms of a disease. We invite you to join us as we walk through this model. And like any journey, it helps to have a compass to guide the way. Here are the four points of our parenting compass.

North: Parenting Is About Managing the Contexts in Which Children Grow and Learn

Parenting is less about managing child behavior and more about managing the contexts in which children live, learn, and play. From a parenting standpoint, the term *context* is not just a place—it could be a relationship, an activity, or an organization. It's anything that occupies a substantial amount of your child's time and attention. It could be something real and concrete, like the school in your neighborhood, or it could be sheer fantasy, like a school for wizards. Some contexts are more positive than others. Some promote healthy development and good citizenship; others are risky, emotionally damaging, or hothouses for emergent delinquent behavior.

With young children, it is relatively easy to manage the contexts of their lives. Parents choose where and with whom they play, what activities are allowed, and how they spend their weekend time. But as children grow older, more of their time is spent away from parents and outside the home, which makes it difficult for parents to have oversight and exert influence. This is especially true for parents of teenagers who might be dating, driving, riding with friends who drive, or hanging out with friends who drink alcohol or smoke marijuana. Sometimes it's all these things.

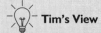 **Tim's View**

When our kids were teenagers and old enough to go out with friends and dating partners, my wife would say to them, "Heat of the moment!" This phrase, which happens to be the title of a hit song by Asia, was my wife's lighthearted way to warn them about making poor decisions in a fit of passion.

Some of the riskier contexts in children's lives are quite appealing, drawing children in despite the risks to their health and development. A classic example is the home where parents are "cool" and allow kids to drink alcohol. Other attractive venues are virtual, such as internet and social media sites where young people gather unsupervised, anonymously, and are only a click away from one another. We can't know all the opportunities that our kids have to engage in unhealthy or risky behavior that seems cool or is modeled by popular peers (e.g., drinking, drug use, unprotected sex). We can easily miss those times when spending the night at a friend's house carries significant risk for delinquent behavior or when a part-time job means having daily contact with kids who use drugs and don't care about school. Even more challenging is when children hide from us the risky but appealing contexts where they spend their time. We ask about these contexts and are told there's nothing to worry about. We ask their friends and get the same answer. We ask *our* friends and get the same answer. But we can track what seems important to our children, what they're drawn to, the key parts of their emerging identity, and where they invest their time and energy. We can also notice the contexts and activities where our children are *not* investing time and energy—time with family, time with schoolwork, and time with old friends.

So, what's a parent to do about risky but attractive contexts that threaten our child's health and development? Should we draw a hard line on our child's independence? When is it time to do that if we can't gauge the level of risk? Our strongest recommendation for how parents can manage contexts that are appealing but risky is **to compete and compete well for your child's time, attention, and respect.** And the best way to compete is with a parent–child relationship that is solid, supportive, and healthy.

South: The Parent–Child Relationship Is the Most Important Context

There are many contexts and environments in which children live, learn, and play, but the parent–child relationship is the most important. It is the primary context in which children learn about life, love, safety, friendships, and their place in the world. It's also a context over which you have some control. Parent–child relationships come with strong emotional ties, enduring roles, recurring interactions, and mutual brain chemistry.

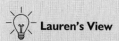 **Lauren's View**

Did you know that when you and your child share an emotional moment that produces feelings such as laughter or love, the same part of the brain lights up in both of you? Or that hugs can produce the "attachment hormone" oxytocin in both you and your child?

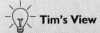

Tim's View

Mental health care providers often refer to therapeutic work with parents as "parent training." I don't like that term. It implies that parents lack parenting skills and thus therapy is simply a matter of them learning new skills for managing their child's behavior. The term also ignores the fact that parents might be living in difficult circumstances or raising challenging kids. Many parents I work with have basic skills but lack a workable plan for how to use those skills to build a healthy relationship with a child who is often hard to manage and hard to like. I prefer to call this work *parent therapy*, akin to couples therapy because its focus is on a relationship going poorly.

For all these reasons, the parent–child relationship is powerful medicine for the many difficulties that families encounter. Scientists are still learning the ways this relationship can benefit children over time. A warm, mutually satisfying parent–child relationship promotes greater cooperation in children and helps them develop a strong sense of right and wrong. A parent–child relationship that is strong and harmonious can be the difference between a child who *might* obey if parents were watching and a child who obeys even when parents are *not* watching.

Research has also shown that strong parent–child relationships are an important protective factor for children who experience traumatic events or high levels of stress. In short, the parent–child relationship is a unique and powerful vessel for sailing the high seas of parenting— and you are its captain.

East: The Parent–Child Relationship Is One Context Among Many That Can Influence Children's Development

Children grow to have many different relationships and increased access to a wide range of contexts over the course of their development. The relationship you have with your child is only one context among many that could influence their lives. For example, research has shown that siblings can exert a powerful influence on children's development. If physically hurting younger siblings gets them to back down or go away, then a child could learn that aggression is a useful strategy for managing conflict. If children see that an older sibling engages in defiant or risky behavior with few consequences, they might be drawn in that same direction. Children also learn via relationships with peers, teachers, extended family members, and many others. Whether it's online video-gaming, sports teams, or social media, all of these contexts have the potential to shape our children's development.

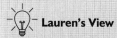 **Lauren's View**

As a new parent, I worried about sending my children to day care. I feared that if they spent several hours each week away from me, it would hurt our relationship. What I found, amazingly, is that each of my children run to me at the end of a long day with a special smile reserved only for me. To see in your children's eyes that you matter to them is a special gift and knowing that my love empowers them to face the world is comforting.

Wise parents try to keep children away from risky contexts. Some might set strict limits on what their children can read, hear, and watch. This approach won't work for all children or all families. It's no small task to limit children's access and exposure to people, places, and things that they consider fun or desirable. Just ask any parent who tries to restrict their teenager's access to friends, to boyfriends or girlfriends, or to screen time. It can be done, but it's not easy and it might not change your child's desire to access contexts that are forbidden but appealing.

POSITIVE CONTEXTS

There are, of course, contexts outside the home that are deserving of children's time and attention. Hopefully, school is one such place.

And despite what you might have heard, most peers push children in positive directions, away from things that parents fear. In fact, *positive peer pressure* can be a parent's best ally during the teen years. Some activities and organizations, depending on how they're run and who is in charge, can offer children rich opportunities for positive development. Unfortunately, some children have limited access to these kinds of positive contexts. Not all children live near places that are safe and fun, offer child-centered activities, and have supportive staff or readily available volunteers. Gaining access to positive contexts can also be costly. Transportation to band or sports practice, musical instruments and sports equipment, and time with a tutor all cost money. Positive developmental contexts are not equal-opportunity employers.

There are also children who struggle to succeed in the positive contexts that are available. They might dress funny, look funny, or talk funny. They might smell bad or do poorly in academics or athletics. They might have trouble following rules. So, when their parents help them access positive developmental contexts, there is no guarantee of acceptance or success. This could mean that parents must also be advocates for their child and support them in their effort to be part of a positive group experience. Parents might need to let their son's teacher know he feels excluded on the playground or remind their daughter's coach that she is enjoying and benefiting from being on the team despite her lack of focus.

Choices

One of the biggest obstacles to managing the contexts of our children's lives is that children make choices, including choices about the contexts in which they invest their time and energy. The choices could be trivial and benign, or they could be serious and risky.

Children might choose to stay in their room, refuse to confide in us, or plan activities outside our home and without our awareness. A certain amount of that is to be expected, and we want our children to be independent. But it's hard to know when they're ready to make *wise* choices about important matters.

West: Managing the Parent–Child Relationship Over Time Is Key

At its core, parenting is a relationship—a relationship between two individuals. Importantly, you're only *one* of those individuals. There is a point at which your skin stops, and your child's skin starts. Parent and child exist as separate beings, each on their own life path. Yes, we're the grown-up in this relationship, but that doesn't mean we can dictate how children will view the relationship or how they will feel toward us. We can't make them respect us—we must earn that. Sure, we can scare them enough that they don't talk back or openly defy us, but that's no guarantee that we'll have a positive influence on them. Children living with dictator-type parents are often the first to drop parents' beliefs and values on the way out the door. We can't unilaterally make the parent–child relationship satisfying or meaningful, but we can recognize the value of working to foster and sustain a strong parent–child relationship.

A Holistic, Long-Term Model of Parenting

A strong parent–child relationship can overcome many of the challenges that arise when a child brings to the world strong emotions and difficult behavior. It's easy to forget that point when you're faced daily with repeated acts of defiance and disobedience, angry bouts of sibling conflict, or a total lack of cooperation with household chores. And too often, these parenting challenges are stacked on top of other demands in your life. When your daughter acts rude or your son ignores you, you're not thinking about your relationship with them; you want them to respect and obey you! But if those behaviors persist or get worse, it could signal a more serious concern—a parent–child relationship that isn't working, that isn't doing the work of guiding children to become healthy, law-abiding adults. Quick solutions to child misbehavior and disrespect are not always the answer; building a strong parent–child relationship is often needed, but that can take time. The core elements of a strong parent–child relationship are parents' capacity to **Accept, Contain,** and **Lead** their child; the supports that underlie and are foundational to parents' efforts to build a strong parent–child relationship are **Goals, Health,** and **Structure** (see Figure 1.1).

Together, these components comprise a six-point plan for good enough parenting. This is a different, holistic way to think about

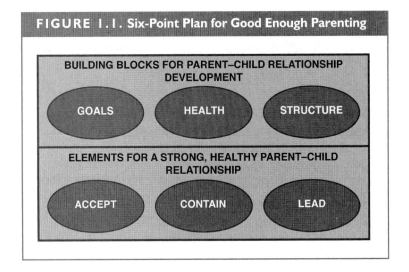

FIGURE 1.1. Six-Point Plan for Good Enough Parenting

BUILDING BLOCKS FOR PARENT–CHILD RELATIONSHIP DEVELOPMENT

GOALS   HEALTH   STRUCTURE

ELEMENTS FOR A STRONG, HEALTHY PARENT–CHILD RELATIONSHIP

ACCEPT   CONTAIN   LEAD

the job of parenting. It recognizes that parenting is important, but also that parents are just one player in the game, and we better be an attractive, competent player. And the best way to compete is through a strong parent–child relationship. Take a moment to consider the kind of relationship you have with your children.

If you're willing, try to answer each of these questions:

- What's going well in the relationship?
- How might your *child* view the relationship?
- How invested is your child in the relationship?
- What's it like to be *your* son or *your* daughter?
- If you were a child, how much *would you respect you?*
- If you were a child, would you follow your example?

 Lauren's View

I often lie in bed at night and wonder, "Was I a good enough parent today? Was my tone too harsh? Was I patient enough?" My husband is good about reminding me how many times I gave them hugs and told them I loved them, how close they cuddled to me when I read to them, and how excited they were to tell me about their day. I might not do everything right, but these moments help me recalibrate. Parenting toddlers is no bed of roses, but it helps when I concentrate on showing my love for them and being someone who they want to be with, share their troubles with, and look to for comfort.

Jason is sitting alone, replaying in his mind his response to Sean during the phone call. Jason is reminded of how his own father yelled at him and what that was like. He also recalls his own desire to move out of the house and away from his father and his overbearing ways. He thinks, hopefully, "Surely, I'm not like him."

Jason then decides to go to Sean, who has been playing quietly but with tears on his cheeks. He looks at his dad but then turns away and wipes his eyes.

Jason doesn't know what to say; he decides to sit on the floor next to Sean, in silence. After a short while, Jason tries to crack a joke but gets no response. Jason then decides to apologize for his angry reaction earlier. Again, Sean is quiet. As Jason leaves the room, he thinks, "This isn't working. I must be the worst parent around."

CHAPTER 2

GOALS: KNOWING WHAT MATTERS IN PARENTING

Consider these two possible truths:

- *Parenting plays a significant role in children's development.*
- *Much of what parents do has little impact on their children's development.*

If both are true, then some parenting actions matter more than others. Research supports that view: Some parenting practices will have little or no effect on children's growth and development, whereas others can make a big difference, especially when repeated over time. Assuming most parents want their children to grow up to be healthy, loving, productive citizens, it would be helpful if parents had a plan, one that emphasized what really matters. It would also be helpful if that plan included important goals to guide parents along the way. With clear goals, parents can know what to pay attention to, when to let go, and where to put their time and energy.

This chapter aims to help you

- define and discuss the impact of risk and protective factors,
- understand and recognize hidden goals,

- introduce the goals important to children's social and emotional development, and
- learn how to set and plan parenting goals.

PARENTING GOALS

What are our goals as a parent? One of the more interesting aspects about parenting is that we seldom stop to ask this question. If we did, we suspect most parents would point to the things they want for their children—being safe, loved, healthy, and content with their life choices. They might also want their children to do well in school, to make friends, to get a job, and to find a caring partner and perhaps have a family. But *none* of these are parenting goals; instead, these are goals parents have for their children, wishes for their children's future.

We use the term *parenting goals* to mean something very specific: These are goals that help parents identify what's important and what matters. Examples include having a loving, accepting relationship with your child or being able to set firm limits on child misbehavior without having to scream angrily or feel out of control. As parents, we're limited in how much control we have over our children's future, but we can control what we say or do in the here and now. So, if we have a clear vision about what's most important in parenting—the things that really matter—we could use that information to guide us, to set clear goals for our parenting. In this way, we have a much better chance of being the kind of parent our children need in their lives. We might also feel better about ourselves, even when things aren't going perfectly.

For most parents, much of what we know about parenting comes from how we were parented and how we saw others being parented. These are valuable sources of information, but science offers something extra and unique—a body of knowledge based on information gathered (and updated and corrected) over multiple studies, involving large numbers of families and using systematic methods of data collection, often conducted over many years. The typical parent doesn't have access to that kind of information. But it's knowledge that can help us know what matters most when it comes to raising children. So, if we're to set parenting goals about things that matter, there's no better resource than the science of how parenting relates to risk and protective factors. This body of scientific information is particularly helpful when selecting the goals of parenting.

THE SCIENCE OF RISK AND PROTECTIVE FACTORS

The science of risk and protective factors can help parents identify factors that affect their child's social and emotional development and set appropriate goals to address them. A *risk factor* is any attribute or characteristic that increases the odds that a child will experience a bad outcome. For example, first-degree relatives of individuals with alcohol use disorder are 2 to 7 times more likely to engage in problem drinking compared with people without relatives with alcohol dependence (National Institute on Alcohol Abuse and Alcoholism, 1997). A *protective factor* is any attribute or characteristic that lowers the odds that a child at risk will experience a bad outcome. For example, researchers have found that children whose parents had alcohol dependence were less likely to develop alcoholic use disorder if their family maintained important family rituals (e.g., family dinners, holidays). Thus, having a parent with alcohol dependence is a risk factor, and living in a family with a parent that preserves important rituals despite having alcohol use disorder appears to be a protective factor.

Research on risk and protective factors tends to confirm what common sense would suggest: Risk factors that predict one problem behavior—say, delinquency—tend to predict other problem behaviors such as academic failure, substance abuse, or high-risk sexual activity. This is because the science of risk and protection is based on what is likely to happen to children *on average*; science cannot reliably predict what will happen in the life of an individual child. Thus, a parent with a coparent with alcohol use disorder could work hard to preserve family rituals and their child could still develop the disorder.

Research Highlight

Research on risk factors and child outcomes began with Sir Michael Rutter's (1989) multidecade study of children born on the Isle of Wight, an island off the coast of England. Rutter's team gathered data from all families on the island who had a child born during a 2-year period in the 1950s. Children's outcomes were assessed periodically over a span of 4 decades (up to age 44–45 years). Rutter created a cumulative risk index across six factors: marital discord, low income, household overcrowding, paternal criminality, maternal psychiatric disorder, and child involvement with foster care. Importantly, there were no differences in outcomes for children in families with none or only one risk factor, but there was a fourfold increase for families with two risk factors and an even greater increase at the level of four or more risk factors.

Although much of the research on youth risk factors has focused on delinquency, parents should also consider risks for various health outcomes (both physical and mental; see Exhibit 2.1). In the United States, rates of adolescent obesity, diabetes, depression, and anxiety are on the rise. Often, youth mental health problems are associated with pressure to achieve academically or be accepted socially. Pressure to achieve, poor physical health, and strained family relationships have all been linked to feelings of chronic stress among

EXHIBIT 2.1. Commonly Cited Risk Factors

Individual

- Early and persistent use of aggression
- Early arrest
- Positive attitudes about antisocial behavior or substance use
- Exposure to violence
- History of trauma, abuse, or neglect
- Victim of discrimination
- Early sexual involvement or teen parenthood
- Excessive pressures to excel
- Psychiatric disorder (attention-deficit/hyperactivity disorder, depression)

Family and/or Parent

- Parent or family history of psychiatric disorder, substance use disorder, or criminality
- Overly permissive or overly punitive discipline
- Poor supervision
- Harsh, rejecting parenting
- Abuse or neglect
- Chaotic or violent family
- Antisocial siblings
- Poverty, unemployment, or frequent moves

School

- Lack of school bonding or low academic engagement
- High-achieving school environment
- Poor relationships with teachers
- Learning problems or low academic achievement
- Frequent absences
- Suspension, expulsion, or dropping out
- Unsafe, unsupportive school climate
- Frequent school changes

(continues)

EXHIBIT 2.1. Commonly Cited Risk Factors (Continued)

Peers

- Rejected, isolated, or bullied by peers
- Associates with deviant peers
- Gang involvement or gang membership

Community

- Neighborhood marked by crime, drugs, and violence
- Access to alcohol, tobacco, and drugs
- Access to firearms
- Fragmented or disorganized community
- Economically disadvantaged neighborhood

---

youth. Indeed, chronic stress can affect teens regardless of family income and has been associated with changes in youths' brain structure, self-esteem, sleep quality, and suicidal ideation.

The science of risk and protection should not be ignored or discounted. For example, one of the more consistent findings from this body of science is that children are protected from adverse childhood experiences when they have a supportive, nurturing relationship with at least one adult in their life. Our hope is that for your children, that adult is you—although we should note that grandparents, teachers, and mentors can also play a pivotal role in promoting your children's growth and development.

Automatic Parenting and Hidden Goals

Much of human behavior is automatic, done with little conscious awareness or mental effort. Some of our behaviors are so ingrained that we don't even think about them. When we drive a car, wash dishes, or get dressed, our mind cruises along and we don't even break a sweat. Automatic behaviors are a real convenience, and we use them all the time. When your daughter asks if she can walk to a friend's house, you don't say, "Hang on. I'll be with you in a second. First, I need to concentrate on folding this towel." Instead, you fold the towel *and* address your daughter, "Sure, honey. Call me when you get there. Be back by 6 for dinner." The way you greet your children in the morning, the way you react when they come home from school, and the way you deal with their misbehavior can all be done in a rather automatic, "programmed" fashion. It's like a button is pushed and your reaction comes out.

Research Highlight

Researchers in Europe asked people questions about going out and socializing to see if this activated the goal of drinking alcohol (Sheeran et al., 2005). The scientists measured how quickly participants responded to the word "drinking" when it was presented very briefly (i.e., 200 milliseconds) on a computer screen as part of a long series of words. Roughly half of the participants were habitual drinkers and half were not. Participants filled out questionnaires before the list of words was presented. Some participants answered questions about socializing with friends (e.g., "Which nights do you go out socializing during a regular week?"), but others answered questions about studying. As expected, those who were habitual drinkers were much quicker to recognize the word "drinking" when first asked about socializing. This was not true when they were asked about studying. For nonhabitual drinkers, the questionnaire they filled out didn't matter. These findings suggest that when individuals are habitual drinkers, simply asking them about socializing can activate the goal of drinking.

Behaviors that are overlearned, automatic, and used repeatedly are what we tend to call *habits*. Habits are incredibly useful; with habits we can perform tasks even while our mind is focused on other, more important things. For example, how often have you driven to work and not remembered what happened along the way? This might be an obvious example, but what is not obvious is that our habits are fueled by goals—goals that are hard to detect. Sigmund Freud believed humans are generally unaware of the motives for the things they do. He called this *unconscious* motivation. Modern science has shown that habits do involve hidden goals, but these goals only become clear in rather challenging situations. The goals that underlie habits are often emotion based, designed to quickly reduce discomfort or some other negative emotional experience.

Parents rely on habits to do much of the work of parenting: to prepare dinner, to manage bedtime, and to get children ready for school. In most instances, that's how it should be. But the goals that drive habits can also mislead parents at times. Imagine a father who believes it's important to show his children that he loves them but who also engages in frequent rants when he comes home from work. Perhaps his hidden goals are a desire for peace and quiet and the chance to relax or to concentrate on work he brought home. If these hidden goals lead to habitual complaining ("Be quiet! You're driving me crazy!"), then his explicit goal to express love to his children will be undermined. If you're a parent who doesn't like feeling disappointed, sad, or anxious, you could find yourself pursuing—again, with little conscious awareness—the goal of minimizing or avoiding those feelings. Your toddler drops her ice cream cone and starts to cry, and you quickly try to silence her tears. You're feeling anxious about your teenager driving, so you pepper her with a dozen questions before and after she runs a brief errand. You're disappointed that your son got such a small part in the school play, so you quiz him about what went "wrong" in the audition. Not only is it hard to see how hidden goals influence our habits, but it's also hard to see how those hidden goals can negatively affect children's development. Instead of helping and supporting our children, we could be inadvertently using a pattern of automatic, negative, emotion-based parenting. Over time, the toddler who drops her ice cream could struggle to handle mistakes and disappointments. Over time, the daughter questioned about her driving could develop fears and doubts about her safety. Over time, the son who got a small part in the play could feel chronically unworthy. We created Worksheet 2.1 to help you recognize goals that could be hiding in your parenting habits.

WORKSHEET 2.1. Hidden Goals That Can Hinder Parenting			
	Yes, It's Me	No, Not Me	Notes
My Dreams: I always wanted to be _____ (examples: an all-star athlete, beauty queen), so I got my children in activities that bring *me* joy. I started them early, hoping one day they win the kind of praise and awards I never did. It would break my heart if they ever wanted to quit.			
My Preferences: I really don't like it when my children show interest in or preference for _____ (e.g., exclusively black clothing, shows like anime), something I can't stand. I discourage them from doing this because I don't want them to be like this as adults.			

(continues)

	Yes, It's Me	No, Not Me	Notes
My Looks: I worry about how my children dress and look. I want others to see them as cute and attractive. I insist that they dress and look good so we can impress others.			
My Worries: I worry something bad will happen to my children, like getting hurt, killed, or abducted. I tell them all the time to be safe and stay close. I do everything I can to protect them. I want them to notice how scared I am.			
My Parenting: I want others to see me as a good parent, someone whose children are smart and well behaved. I get angry when they act up in public and embarrass me.			
My Authority: It's important that my children show me respect. I don't like backtalk or sass. I don't want to see attitude or eye rolls. I shouldn't have to ask them twice to do something.			

WORKSHEET 2.1. Hidden Goals That Can Hinder Parenting (*Continued*)	Yes, It's Me	No, Not Me	Notes
My Feelings: My children should know when I'm not feeling my best. They should behave and not make things worse when I'm mad or sad. If they were good, they would leave me alone or try to comfort me.			
My Comfort: I hate when my kids are upset and crying. I try right away to make things better. I tell them not to cry or scream, that there's no reason to be upset.			

Explicit Parenting Goals

Parents who recognize that hazards that come with overreliance on habitual, automatic parenting could opt to be more intentional. For example, they could vow to pause, reflect, and consider their options before reacting. A purpose-driven, problem-solving approach to parenting can certainly be helpful, but it can also be difficult to use on a regular basis. Researchers tell us that our ability to override automatic behaviors by consciously selecting and using "on-purpose" behaviors is limited; we can do it for a short while, but eventually other things occupy our mind and automatic behaviors take over once again. So, we can't think, plan, or will our way out of every parenting dilemma. Instead, we must manage the factors that influence our automatic parenting. One of those is our overall health and well-being (which is the topic of the next chapter). Another is our choice of parenting goals. By setting clear, explicit goals, we can better avoid parenting missteps, even when parenting is automatic.

The science of parenting and child development can help identify the kinds of goals that are important for parents who seek to enhance their child's social and emotional development. Ideally, parenting is a means of promoting children's capacity for relatedness, autonomy, and competence. *Relatedness* refers to children's sense of belonging and connection to others. *Autonomy* refers to children's ability to act on their own behalf and to have a sense of personal control. *Competence* is the ability to effectively interact with and adapt to one's environment. Children who have these abilities will more likely grow up to be resilient teenagers and adults.

Not surprisingly, researchers find that children who struggle with relatedness, autonomy, and competence tend to have more problematic outcomes. Consider, for example, children who use aggression, coercion, or strong emotional displays to influence others. None of these, if used repeatedly, are healthy forms of relating to or interacting with others. Consider also children who cope by being really passive, allowing things to happen without any action or responsibility on their part. Instead of developing a sense of autonomy and personal control, these children will likely depend on others to meet their needs. Finally, consider children who pull back from (or are repeatedly shielded from) difficult life challenges and the opportunity to learn important, basic skills. Because this could limit their development of fundamental skills and competencies, these children will likely struggle to adapt to life's ups and downs. Some child outcomes depend largely on their genes (e.g., first-chair tuba player, gifted intellectual, comedian), but parenting is an important determinant of whether children develop relatedness, autonomy, and competence. In short, **there's an important job for parents to do.** Therefore, it's vital that parents are intentional about doing the important work of parenting and avoid drifting into the pursuit of hidden, emotion-based goals that are not tied to essential outcomes.

As noted in Chapter 1, our holistic, long-term model of parenting views goals as one component in a solid plan for parenting: the **six-point plan for good enough parenting** (see Worksheet 2.2). For now, our recommendation is to consider the possibility that

WORKSHEET 2.2. Six-Point Plan for Good Enough Parenting

	Yes, It's Me	No, Not Me	Notes
1. Goals: I make clear, explicit goals for parenting and try to be aware of emotion-driven goals that are hiding in my automatic parenting habits.			
2. Health: I prioritize my emotional health because it's essential to maintaining the strength, energy, and commitment needed for parenting.			
3. Structure: I use the 4 Rs (routines, roles, rules, and rituals) to give my home/family the structure it needs.			

(continues)

WORKSHEET 2.2. Six-Point Plan for Good Enough Parenting (Continued)

	Yes, It's Me	No, Not Me	Notes
4. Accept: I give my children room to make choices *and* mistakes, I notice and validate what they feel, and I'm curious about their thoughts, worries, and dreams.			
5. Contain: I limit my children's use of aggression and coercion by being consistent, firm, and selective with my discipline, and I reconnect with them afterward.			
6. Lead: I give my children an example to respect and follow, and I openly share with them the values and beliefs that guide my behavior.			

parenting can significantly improve if we set clear, specific goals for parenting that are guided by our good enough parenting plan.

Setting and Using Parenting Goals

Goals are powerful tools that can help make parenting less draining and more rewarding for you and your children. Maybe looking at these goals helps provide some clarity and direction. Maybe you are wondering where to start. The simplest way is by creating a new habit—one that involves taking time on a regular basis (every week or month) to consider whether your parenting is meeting each of these goals. By reminding yourself of key parenting goals, you're less likely to drift toward the hidden, habitual, emotion-driven parenting goals we discussed earlier. Instead, you'd be interacting with your children in a purposeful way that is informed by the science.

Of course, you will have times when you're not sure which parenting goal is most relevant to a given situation. You could even find your parenting goals are in conflict with one another. You may have to decide between communicating a message of acceptance to your son now or setting a firm limit on his behavior. In another instance, you may have to choose between dropping your family's dinner routine one night and doing something that is in line with your family's values instead (e.g., helping with your daughter's school fundraiser). As we pointed out at the start of this book, our aim is *not* to offer ready-made answers for every parenting dilemma or child misbehavior. We can't accurately say whether [insert child behavior here] should be met with [insert parent response here] without knowing the context for this interaction and the history of the parent–child relationship. Parenting and life are not that simple, and all six aspects of good enough parenting are important: Three represent the essential components of a healthy parent–child relationship (Accept, Contain, Lead) and three represent the foundational supports needed to sustain a healthy parent–child relationship (Goals, Health, Structure). All are important in promoting and maintaining a healthy parent–child relationship over time, which is parents' best tool when children are struggling to develop the capacity for relatedness, autonomy, and competence.

EXAMPLE: CHORES VERSUS FRIENDS

Here's an example of how parents might sort through a situation in which there are competing parenting goals. Your son is hanging out with friends, watching TV and playing video games. They're not too loud or making a mess, but you realize that your son hasn't done his chores. It's almost time for dinner; after that, he'll need time to do his homework. Do you send his friends home so he can get his chores done before dinner, *or* do you let him slide on the chores because his friends don't come to his house that often? How would you choose between these two actions? What other factors you should consider? Some parenting experts would advise you to address first the "problem behavior" of your son not doing his chores. But we can imagine that some parents would question the wisdom of sending his friends home and insisting he do his chores. They might ask, "Is that really necessary or helpful right now?" Of course, those same parents might wonder later if they were giving in and failing to use "effective parenting?"

How does this fit with our six-point plan for good enough parenting? How does your son's failure to do his chores in this situation fit the long-term goal of growth and development? What if not doing his chores was a long-standing problem? What if his friends were the type to pressure him into delinquent activity? If you were to send his friends home and insist he do his chores, you might still be viewed as the "bad guy," but that decision—under these circumstances—seems very much in line with the parenting goals we've outlined in this book. But if your son reliably did his chores and his friends seldom caused any trouble for their parents or teachers, then letting him slide on chores in this situation could be a way to help him become more accepted by a group of positive, prosocial peers.

Now imagine that your relationship with your son was strained and that he seems to have little respect for you. Under these circumstances, conflict with your son, especially in front of his friends, could escalate rather quickly. So, should you let him slide, even if he wasn't great about doing his chores and his friends weren't the best influence on him? This is a much more challenging situation:

Your efforts to limit your son's involvement in problem behavior could collide mightily with your efforts to repair the parent–child relationship. Both are important. Because we view the parent–child relationship as the most important context and your most powerful tool in parenting, we would suggest that takes precedent. But what does that look like? It could mean pulling your son aside, reminding him privately about his chores, but letting him slide this time. If you were to do this, you let him know the relationship you two have is important but so are his chores. He'll still try to avoid chores in the future, but he'll appreciate the fact that you didn't call him out in front of his friends. And recognize that you're not yet done in righting your relationship with your son. More work is needed. It might mean greater acceptance, better containment, or a healthier example for him to follow—or perhaps all three. Regardless, the goal of building a healthy parent–son relationship should always come first, even before important issues such as chores and the likely influence of negative peers.

You can see from this one scenario how complicated parenting can get. It's worth pointing out that none of that complexity came from a lack of parenting skills. Instead, the complexity comes from parents needing to identify what matters most in their effort to be good enough parents.

Minimum Coverage With Maximum Sustainability

The parent–child relationship—when managed well over time—can have a tremendous influence on your children's development. Often overlooked in this claim is the "over time" part. Remember, parenting is a long-term gig. Therefore, an important question parents should be asking is this: "What strategies give me the best chance that I can accept, contain, and lead my children for 18-plus years?" Our recommendation is to use a strategy that offers *minimum coverage* but *maximum sustainability* of parents' capacity to accept, contain, and lead. We discuss later what that looks like, but for now recognize that there are lots of ways to do each of these. There is not one way to use this plan, so there's no need to choose an approach that is overly cumbersome and unsustainable. That's what can happen when parents are wedded to a particular list of parenting skills or to a highly prescriptive model of parenting. If you have trouble maintaining your efforts to accept, contain, and lead, then you'll need strategies that are more workable and flexible. There's still the need for "minimal coverage," but in the chapters that follow, you'll learn about ways to parent that are both sustainable and provide at least minimal coverage of the conditions needed to raise healthy, productive citizens.

GOALS HOMEWORK

Now that you've learned about the importance of parenting goals, it's time to practice being thoughtful about making your parenting goals clear and explicit. Awareness is the first step in changing a behavior, especially a parenting behavior that is now automatic. It can help to look for patterns, moments when you interacted with your child and felt disheartened or incompetent. Keep track and write them down. Look for any similarities in situations that leave you feeling discouraged or ineffective, then consider potential underlying, emotion-based goals that might be operating. Now consider how this pattern fits or doesn't fit with the other components in our good enough parenting plan. Which aspects of our good enough parenting plan should become your current parenting goals?

Here's an example: You notice your son has been reluctant to share information with you. You think it's because you need to be more accepting. So, the next time he complains or makes a whiny comment, you have in your mind the goal of being more accepting instead of making a sarcastic comeback ("Yeah, your life is so hard"). You offer this response: "It sounds like a tough time for you right now." See if you can alter your pattern of parenting by adopting new and different goals. Here are other homework tasks you can do:

1. Review Worksheet 2.1, which lists hidden goals that can hurt parenting.
2. Review Worksheet 2.2, which lists the six-point plan to good enough parenting.
3. Rate yourself on the extent to which each type of goal is shaping your parenting.
4. Commit to revisiting each month or two the specific goals that drive your parenting.

CHAPTER 3

HEALTH: AN ESSENTIAL INGREDIENT IN PARENTING

Talking with parents about how their health affects parenting is not easy. The risk is that parents will hear these conversations as judgment, criticism, or cluelessness. And if we're being truly honest, we'd have to admit there are likely times when, unknowingly, what we say to parents can sound judgmental, critical, or clueless. Thus, with humility and lots of trepidation, we begin this chapter with a sample of what these conversations are like. We usually start by explaining that we use the word *health* in its broadest sense ("Health with a capital H"), meaning that it's meant to cover multiple areas of functioning: physical, mental, emotional, relational, occupational, familial, sexual, and spiritual forms of health and well-being. We would note, however, that in this book, we are mostly concerned with parents' emotional health. We also use the term *self-care*, which usually means keeping track of your health status and caring for yourself as needed. Here's a sample of how these conversations might go:

> *Us:* It doesn't sound like you have much time to yourself—time to stop, catch your breath, and collect your thoughts.
>
> *Parent:* Are you kidding? I don't have time to go to the bathroom!

Us: Does it help when you do get a break or have some time off? Parents who struggle with child-rearing tell us it can help, especially if they know when that break is coming and they don't have to wait too long for the next one.

Parent: Oh, I'd love to go to a movie, or visit a friend, or just watch TV without being interrupted every 5 seconds. But that's not going to happen.

Us: Is that because it seems impossible or because you're not sure it'd help, or perhaps because you'd feel guilty doing it?

Parent: I might feel a little guilty, but mainly it's because I don't have the time.

Us: So, how do you do it? How do you keep going, day in and day out, with all you have to do as a parent, without a break?

Parent: I don't know. I guess because I have to. No one else is going to do it. Every once in a while, I ask my mom to watch the kids, but it's usually not worth the hassle . . . Maybe when my kids finally finish school. Ha-ha!

Us: Will you make it until then?

Parent: I have to!

Us: But how? I'm wondering if helping yourself in some way can help both you and your children?

Parent: I'm not sure what you mean.

Us: Children look up to, respect, and imitate adults who they see as healthy, strong, and caring. So, one of the best ways to help your children is to be the healthiest parent you can be. I see how caring you are, but kids also benefit when their parents are strong and

> healthy. That means taking care of yourself
> physically and emotionally, perhaps by making
> small changes in how you care for yourself,
> how you see yourself, and, eventually, how
> your children see you. I hope we can talk
> about what that might look like.

The main point of this chapter is not that being healthy is good for parents; it's that *health is an essential ingredient in parenting.* This is something of a paradox: If parents spend time dealing with their own health and well-being, won't that interfere with the job of parenting? Perhaps. But if you're a parent who pays attention to your health, then you know how important health can be to parenting. You also probably know much of what's in this chapter. Some parents might be surprised to learn that health is a big part of parenting, and others might have heard this but are unsure of how to balance parenting and self-care. We also imagine that there are still other parents who believe parental self-care is silly or selfish.

This chapter aims to help you

- learn why health, especially emotional health, is an essential ingredient in parenting,
- conduct an inventory of your health,
- learn how to use emotions wisely,
- diversify your "portfolio" of self-care and coping, and
- learn how to practice mindfulness.

WHY IS HEALTH AN ESSENTIAL INGREDIENT IN PARENTING?

In his book on the seven habits of highly effective people, Stephen Covey (1991) told the tale of a man laboring to cut down trees. When a passerby suggests that he sharpen his saw, the man says he's too busy cutting down trees to sharpen his saw! **The same is often true for parents.** It's hard to feel like you have the time or the resources to make self-care a priority, but health is an essential ingredient to the long-term job of parenting. Yes, there are lots of barriers that stand in the way, but unhealthy parents have a tougher time promoting their children's growth and development than do healthy parents. Therefore, our first aim in this chapter is to help you understand why health is an essential ingredient in parenting.

One thing that makes health so important is that parenting is a one-sided, *vertical* relationship. It's vertical in that adults carry most of the responsibility—children depend on parents much more than parents depend on children. Relationships between siblings or peers are said to be *horizontal* because there's an expectation of equal power and mutual dependence. Because parenting is a vertical relationship, parents can grow weary and at times feel burned out and overwhelmed. As parents, we will give more than we get for many years, so we can't rely on our children to make us feel better or to give meaning and significance to our life. That is especially true if our children are experiencing emotional or behavioral difficulties.

ENERGY, STRENGTH, AND COMMITMENT

The vertical nature of the parent–child relationship means parents can't ignore their own health. They need a plan for monitoring and managing their health while still doing the job of parenting. It's not enough to be smart and know a lot; parents also need **energy, strength,** and **commitment.** These are the main gifts that health brings to parenting.

Energy

The core message of this book is that parenting, at its heart, is a relationship—a long-term relationship that has the potential to greatly influence children's growth and development. But it's also a one-sided relationship. Children need parents to care about them and to invest in their lives, but that can be hard and draining and sometimes parents lack the energy to do the job. Like automobiles, parents need to refuel, or they won't have the energy to sustain themselves. When parents are depressed, overwhelmed, overworked, chronically stressed, or isolated from family and friends, they are more likely to run out of fuel. Parents of difficult, strong-willed children are also at risk for low energy and for feeling burned out. Parents need reliable and practical ways to refuel, to be heard and understood, to feel supported by other adults, and to get the rest and nutrition their body needs.

Strength

Staying with our earlier car analogy, the concept of parental strength is akin to a vehicle's horsepower: A fully fueled car might not be up to the task if it lacks horsepower, which is the power or strength to pull its load. Strength helps parents make

 Lauren's View

Parents' emotional health is like a bucket, and every stressful event is like a cup of water poured into that bucket. A single stressful event is no big deal, but when stress builds up, both parents and parenting can suffer. Imagine that the junior high school counselor calls to say your daughter has been late to math class 2 days in a row, and then you learn that evening that your air conditioner is not working. Some stressful events can't be predicted, but efforts to manage stress can be predicted if scheduled. By building stress-reducing activities into your schedule, you're not waiting until you're feeling overwhelmed to do something about stress. Instead, dates on a calendar (e.g., every Friday, first weekend of the month) are your cues to be proactive so you can take some water out of your stress bucket.

timely sacrifices and follow through with unpopular parenting decisions like setting firm limits and enforcing family rules. Strength also helps parents act wisely when children protest or have emotional meltdowns, when others might be critical of their parenting, or when life's demands are adding up too quickly. Your strength as a parent often depends on the depth of your character or your personal integrity. Character and integrity are influenced by many factors, including your personality traits (e.g., hope, resilience), your childhood experiences, and your current life circumstances. When you are parenting a difficult strong-willed child, strength is what enables you to do the wise thing, even when there's interference from opposing forces, external and internal. External forces include your children's protests and counterattacks, the doubts and criticisms of other adults, and the competing demands of your busy life. Internal forces include your own doubts and self-criticisms as well as the emotional costs that arise when you carry out unpopular executive decisions.

Commitment

Commitment, when driving your metaphorical parenting car, is essentially choosing the direction you are driving. Ideally, the direction we take our family is determined by our values. *Values* are the answers we give to the really big questions in life: Do we want a life partner? Do we want to have and raise children? What do we want for our work life: caring for home and family, making money, working with our hands, or healing others? Is spirituality an important part of our life? Should we engage in public service and efforts to support community? How important is physical exercise, recreation, and travel to other places? We assume that if you're reading this book, then one of your values is being a capable, caring parent.

YOUR HEALTH INVENTORY

Who do *you* talk to about your health? In the United States, health care is quite advanced, and yet it can be hard to find time to talk about your health with someone who truly listens and cares. When we meet with our primary care doctor, we're encouraged to get right to the problem, with little time left over for "visiting." Some parents rarely go to the doctor, while some can't even afford to; others aren't comfortable talking about health-related concerns or don't feel respected by their doctor, which is more common among people of color. There are also parents whose body size or shape is likely to mean that health-related discussions are experienced as lectures about diet, exercise, and the need for "lifestyle changes."

We want you to have an opportunity to take stock of your health. Worksheet 3.1 is what we call "Your Health Inventory," which is just a fancy name for a long list of areas in life that could signal better or worse health. Remember, we use "Health" with a capital H to mean more than physical health or medical problems. You can grade each area with A, B, C, D, or F, just like in school. Use this inventory to gauge your overall level of health and to identify areas that might need more attention. We don't have a system for scoring this inventory, but we do assume that healthier folks will circle more As or Bs than Ds or Fs.

Please use your judgment when "grading" each of the worksheet items. There will be big differences in the meaning of these items from one person to the next. Some items simply won't apply to you. For example, not all care about spirituality, lots of folks don't have a romantic partner, and some people work alone and don't have coworkers. Also, keep in mind that spending time with others can be health promoting *or not*. Some "friends" are not very friendly, and not all family members have your best interest in mind. In fact, some parents are probably healthier because they *ended*

How would you "grade" each of the following areas, at this point in your life?

Your physical health	A	B	C	D	F
Your mental abilities	A	B	C	D	F
Your emotional and psychological health	A	B	C	D	F
Your spiritual health	A	B	C	D	F
Your marriage or romantic relationships	A	B	C	D	F
Your relationships with your children	A	B	C	D	F
Your relationships with adult family members	A	B	C	D	F
Your relationships with neighbors	A	B	C	D	F
Your relationships with coworkers	A	B	C	D	F
Your relationships with adult friends	A	B	C	D	F
Your involvement with groups or organizations	A	B	C	D	F
Your hobbies/leisure time	A	B	C	D	F
Your entertainment activities	A	B	C	D	F
Your recreational/exercise activities	A	B	C	D	F
Your work outside the home	A	B	C	D	F
Your chores in the home	A	B	C	D	F
Your financial situation	A	B	C	D	F
The home or apartment where you live	A	B	C	D	F
Your neighborhood	A	B	C	D	F

relationships with friends and family members who only criticize and pass judgment.

Parent Health Concerns

Poor parent health can take many forms. Some parents have chronic medical conditions, such as hypertension, diabetes, or respiratory illness, whereas others suffer from recurring mental health or substance use problems. Each of these conditions can interfere with or disrupt parenting. It is also true that parenting is generally easier and more satisfying when parents are well rested, are adequately nourished, and have opportunities to exercise. Sleep, nutrition, and movement are basic health needs, but some parents don't get enough sleep, some find it hard to eat healthy, and some don't have time or desire to exercise. We recognize that sacrifice is a part of parenting, but we encourage parents not to sacrifice their need for sleep, nutrition, and movement. This is especially true for sleep: Parents can tolerate sleep problems for a short while, but poor sleep can have a negative impact on many other aspects of physical and mental health.

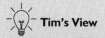 **Tim's View**

The American Sleep Association (n.d.) suggests these tips for better sleep:

1. Go to bed around the same time and wake up around the same time each day.
2. Avoid daytime naps.
3. Don't stay in bed awake for more than 5 to 10 minutes.
4. If that happens, sit in the dark and don't go back to bed until you're sleepy.
5. Don't watch television, use the computer, or read in bed.
6. Limit your use of caffeinated drinks such as coffee, tea, and soda.
7. Cigarettes, alcohol, and over-the-counter medications can disrupt sleep.
8. Avoid rigorous exercise before bedtime.
9. Sleep in a room that is cool, quiet, dark, and has plenty of fresh air.
10. If you are a "clock watcher" at night, hide the clock.

EMOTIONS AND PARENTING

Our reading of the research suggests that poor emotional health is the most common determinant of problems in parenting. This makes sense given that parenting is first and foremost a relationship. Poor emotional health is a hazard for nearly all meaningful, close relationships but especially so for vertical relationships such as parenting in which children depend on adults. Think about what motivates you as a parent. Why do you do it, day after day, for so many years? Evolutionary scientists tell us that having children is nature's way of making sure our DNA survives for another generation. Behaviorists tell us that parenting, like all behavior, is shaped by its consequences, positive and negative. If that's true, then what are the rewards of parenting? Few get rich from being a parent unless their son is a first-round draft pick in the NBA. And when children are young, parents have very little free time; many would say their love life suffered once they took on the role of parenting. Therefore, the payoffs for parenting tend to be more emotional in nature. When we bring children into the world and into our homes, when we witness their growth and development over time, there's a good chance we'll experience feelings of joy, love, and excitement as well as a sense of pride. But, of course, we're also likely to experience other feelings, some that are less comfortable such as fear, sadness, disappointment, and hurt. In other words, the job of parenting is likely to generate a range of feelings and thoughts, some that are unwanted or uncomfortable.

Fortunately for our species, most humans seem to believe that having and raising children adds meaning and value to their life. One way we know parenting is meaningful is that it shows up in how we feel. There's no way to talk about the rewards of parenting without talking about the feelings we get as parents. Dads witness the miracle of childbirth and are exhilarated. Moms hold their squeaky clean, just-bathed toddler, breathe in the sweet smell of their child's tiny head, and feel boundless love and affection. A family plays together in the park, and everyone experiences bursts of surprise and joy. Children grow, share, sing, play, learn, achieve, and fall in love—all the while we watch, delighting in the pride that only a parent can feel. Feelings are a key upside to parenting. Of course, feelings are also a common downside to parenting. This is especially true in families with strong-willed children where parenting can seem like an endless series of emotional battles.

Emotions 101

Writer Elizabeth Stone had it right when she said choosing to be a parent is to decide forever to have your heart go walking around outside your body. So, if we're going to discuss how health can affect your parenting, we must talk about emotions. Here's a formal definition of *emotions*: Emotions are subjective states of arousal that combine (a) our initial perception of an event, (b) our body and our brain's initial reaction to that perception, and (c) our brain's secondary appraisal of what happened and how we reacted to it. As humans, we are hardwired to perceive almost instantly if an event is a threat, a desired object, an obstacle in our way, or something completely new and different. The body's early warning system triggers an initial response that engages the face as well as the autonomic nervous system, the part of our body that prepares us for fight or flight. Following right behind these first-alert reactions is the mind's attempt to make sense of what is happening. We call this rapid-fire experience an emotion or a feeling. Typically, after a few minutes, the feeling will go away. Here are the 10 most useful facts about your emotions:

1. Emotions contain information we can use.
2. Emotions contain information others can use.
3. We can feel an emotion and not act on it.

4. We can act emotionally and not feel it.
5. Emotions are unpredictable consequences of our actions.
6. Negative emotions are unpleasant and perfectly normal.
7. Emotions don't cause problems; avoiding emotions causes problems.
8. Emotions are subjective and temporary.
9. Admitting fear, sadness, and shame is helpful; venting, fretting, and rumination are less helpful.
10. Managing emotions and managing relationships go hand in hand.

These are facts parents can use every day, and we discuss each in more detail next.

EMOTIONS CONTAIN INFORMATION WE CAN USE

In our experience, the notion that emotions contain information we can use is a well-kept secret. People readily welcome positive emotions such as joy or love, but too often we are programmed to turn away from feelings of sadness, fear, disappointment, and other "negative" emotions. These kinds of internal experiences are neither invited nor wanted; we cast them as problems that require immediate elimination or escape. And yet, one of the more well-established truths in mental health is that avoiding emotions tends to cause more problems than feeling our feelings (see Fact 7).

Try this brief exercise. Close your eyes, take a few slow deep breaths, and try to remember a specific parenting event, something that happened and stayed with you because it still hurts or left you with nagging doubts or fears. Try to visualize your memory of this event in your mind's eye: Picture where it occurred, who was there, and what you and others were doing and wearing. Pay attention to whatever details and images pop into your mind. Recalling this kind of memory could mean "re-feeling" the emotions of the event. If that happens, try to lean into and linger just a bit on those emotions. See if you can wait long enough to experience what happens when you're not trying to escape the emotional impact of an event. The idea of this exercise is to practice being open to the emotions that come with the events of our lives. Few of us do this routinely. Instead, if we don't like how we feel after an event, we try to change how we feel, often rather quickly. But consider what would happen if you leaned into unpleasant emotional experiences, waiting to see which emotions showed up. At this point, we assume you're asking yourself, "Why would anyone in their right mind do that?"

The answer lies in the fact that emotions, even the unpleasant ones, contain information we can use. Fear "tells" a dad it's dangerous for his 3-year-old to run through a parking lot, so it's important to watch for cars. Anger "tells" a mom it's wrong for her 15-year-old to call her a b*!$^, so it's important to discuss this with her daughter. But not all parenting situations carry clear emotional messages. More common is experiencing a confusing mix of feelings, often stacked like rocky layers with the most intense or most familiar emotion sitting on top, inviting action. Parents might respond quickly when they're angry but later recognize there were other feelings that were part of that hot mess of emotions. These could be hurt, disappointment, sadness, or even shame. And how we respond when we're hurt or sad is likely to be very different from how we respond if we're angry. That's why it's so helpful to lean into and learn from our emotions. It might seem silly, especially if you're a parent who often feels anxious or stressed, but the scientific evidence here is quite solid. When we take the time to feel our feelings (rather than spend energy on suppressing our feelings), we can access information we can use to be better parents.

Keep in mind that the information we get from our feelings is rather limited; it's not enough to plan fully how we should act. But if we add emotion information to what we already know and what we've learned in the past, we can act more wisely. Feelings are merely nudges that push us in one direction or another. With the information we gain from them, we can do a better job of relating to those we love. Sometimes our emotional response is so strong that we shift immediately into fight-or-flight mode, the body's primitive mechanism for keeping us safe in the face of a threat. Feelings that come with a fight-or-flight response are more like a big shove than a subtle nudge, and they're harder to ignore. But with practice, we can learn to use the information in our emotions rather than have our emotions use us, and we can do a better job of relating to those we love.

Imagine being the mother whose teenage daughter called her a b*!$^. How would you feel if that were you? Mad? Hurt? Shocked? Confused? Disappointed? All are possible, depending on the relationship you have with your daughter, and there isn't likely to be a single, solitary feeling that shows up. Instead, it's likely a variety pack of feelings. However, by spending just a bit of time feeling your feelings, you can find the ones that are most compelling. You might find them "hiding" under your anger or behind your shock, the feelings that arrive more quickly and louder. This means you'll have to feel angry or shocked before you can get to these underlying important emotions. Your response to your teenage daughter in this scenario will vary depending on which emotion you use. Perhaps you'll focus on feeling hurt, sad, or even fearful about what this event means for your relationship going forward. If you did focus on feeling sad or fearful rather than angry, how might your words to her differ? What might we say to our child if we feel sad or frightened versus simply angry? Which emotion is likely to lead to the kind of words that benefit your daughter and your relationship with her?

Emotions Contain Information Others Can Use

Charles Darwin (1859/2004) theorized that before there was human language, facial expressions helped us (and nonhuman animals) survive as a species because they communicated alarm and other useful information to others. When Joe Caveman spat out a chunk of food and made a face that we'd call "disgust," other cavepersons knew to steer clear of the tainted food. Today, we have the gift of spoken and written language, but in some ways we're not much better at communicating our feelings. The greeting card industry knows this all too well. Consider the kinds of cards marketed to men; almost all begin with the giver admitting he is not good at putting feelings into words. Perhaps these cards are appealing because they remind romantic partners not to expect too much on the feelings front (and, oh yeah, Happy Birthday or Happy Anniversary). However, men convey emotional information in other ways—a tight jaw, a strained voice, watery eyes, or a sudden bolt out the door. Of course, it's not just men who do these things. It's also women, and boys and girls, and yes, parents.

If parents are to use their emotions to inform others, including their children, they must first learn to use emotions to inform themselves (as discussed earlier). When parents feel their feelings and seek the information contained in those feelings, they can more effectively and gently convey important emotion information to their children. But when emotional information is "leaked out," perhaps nonverbally, the message to children is not very clear. It can arrive garbled, mixed, or incomplete. Instead of learning that Mom felt hurt and taken for granted when her son made a mess in the kitchen, he only hears anger and rejection. Instead of learning that Dad is concerned about his daughter's safety when she resumes dating a questionable ex-boyfriend, she only hears criticism and lecturing. Emotionally charged messages like, "I can't believe you're so stupid!" or "Dammit! I told you this would happen!" can be transformed into softer messages like these: "I love you. I really do. But right now, I'm really frustrated," or "I'm sorry. I was just so disappointed. Let me explain."

Notice what's different about these "transformed" emotional messages: They are not preprogrammed *I* statements delivered robotically after counting to 10 (although that's not a terrible option). These messages are an honest report of what parents felt but delivered after first spending time feeling their feelings. A parent narrating this whole process might sound like this:

> I'm not liking how I feel right now. I'm feeling a mix of emotions and I'm being nudged in many different directions. Part of me wants to lash out, but I also feel like crying, quitting, giving up, and hurting back.

Wise parents read their emotions like a thermostat on the wall and find a way to tell others what they learned in a nonhurtful way. Especially useful are *I* statements that describe what *they* are feeling and what it means for others. Parents who practice these steps are giving a tremendous gift to themselves, to their children, and to the parent–child relationship. Accurately sharing emotion information won't eliminate times when emotions get the best of you, but it certainly helps to have options for limiting the damaging effects of strong, emotion-driven parenting.

We Can Feel an Emotion and Not Act on It

You've probably heard the term *anger management*, which was coined in the mid-1970s. A common misconception is that anger causes aggression and other forms of violence, so to reduce aggression we should reduce anger. But there's not a simple, one-to-one correspondence between anger and aggression. We are all quite capable of feeling angry without being aggressive. Yes, folks who are really mad are more likely to act aggressively than folks who are not mad, but anger is rarely a single, powerful *cause* of aggression. Anger can set the stage for aggression, but we don't become so incapacitated by anger that we lose all control over our actions. Consider the child whose "out of control" anger leads to slammed doors and damaged walls but not to hurt family members. The ability to have a feeling and not act on it is not limited to anger and it's not limited to children. Emotions can definitely affect how *well* or how *poorly* we do something, but emotions don't change us into hypnotized robots. In almost every instance, we retain the option of feeling the emotion without acting on it. Here's a useful reminder, for both parents and children: Just because you feel _____ [angry, sad, etc.], doesn't mean you can _____ [do something hurtful].

We Can Act Emotionally and Not Feel It

Humans are great imitators, and one of things we can imitate is an emotional reaction—even if there's no real underlying emotional experience. Professional actors get paid to do this, perhaps drawing on past emotional experiences to portray a "present" emotional reaction. But actors aren't the only ones who learn to act out an emotion that is not fully felt. Some of us learn to use this strategy: "I'm falling apart and can't stand it, so you better rescue me." Others learn this strategy: "I'm really mad and will hurt somebody, so you better do what I say." These are not "faked" emotions used with an intent to deceive; rather, these are *instrumental emotions* that likely began as a way to manage strong feelings but then morphed into a tool for influencing others. Over time, it becomes harder to tell the difference between instrumental emotions and authentic emotions. In general, others can tell better than us if our emotional reactions are being used as an influence tool, although family members are usually more susceptible to the pull of emotion-based influence strategies than nonfamily members.

63

Families can suffer when unreasonable demands are packaged inside strong emotional displays. It's bad enough when kids do this; it's particularly toxic when parents do it. Imagine a mom inconvenienced by her daughter's plan to go to her friend's house. Despite her daughter having made a plan and getting prior consent, this mom is responding to the inconvenience with a show of anger that scares her daughter into staying home. Or perhaps this mom shows hurt and sadness that leaves her daughter feeling guilty about not staying home. Either way, it won't be easy for the daughter to recognize and address her mom's unreasonable demands. Not many children can say, "Mom, I know it's inconvenient for me to go to my friend's house, and I see that you're hurt and angry. But you'll be fine, and we agreed earlier that what I'm doing is reasonable." A coparent *might* be able to deliver that message to a parent, but even that would come with a risk of being seen as undermining parental authority.

If you think you're a parent who uses emotions to unfairly influence your children, talk with an adult who knows you well and ask them for honest, constructive feedback. You might say it this way: "Do you ever see me becoming emotional to get my way, maybe by looking sad, making others feel guilty, or scaring them with my anger?" Second, think about times when you showed anger, fear, or sadness around your children. Look for any patterns in your use of these emotional displays. You could even ask them what it's like when they see you angry, scared, or sad. If you sense that you might be using emotional displays as an influential tool, consider how you can put into words what you feel, want, or need in those situations instead.

EMOTIONS ARE UNPREDICTABLE CONSEQUENCES OF OUR ACTIONS

Our actions usually lead to certain consequences, some that are predictable and some that are not predictable. When our behavior leads consistently to positive consequences, we tend to repeat it. When our behavior leads to consequences that are consistently negative, we're less likely to repeat it. Our emotions are one consequence of our actions, byproducts of what we do and what we say, where we go, and who we meet. We like when our actions and our words lead to positive emotions such as joy, pride, or affection, but we can't always know which emotions will show up because of our actions. Of course, we all have strategies for generating positive emotions (e.g., phoning a friend) and for trying to minimize negative emotions (e.g., drinking alcohol), but ultimately, our emotions are not entirely under conscious control. We can't immediately and intentionally produce positive emotions and we can't immediately and intentionally dismiss negative emotions, despite our desire to do so. We hear clients say: "There's no reason for me to feel that way" or "I just want to be happy," puzzled that some feelings arrive unannounced and unwanted. Some people search their whole lives for sure-fire ways to experience positive emotions or to escape negative emotions. But trying to control our emotions is often illusory and harmful.

Negative Emotions Are Unpleasant and Perfectly Normal

In his widely read self-help book, Harold Kushner asked, "Why do bad things happen to good people?" Kushner (2007) offered a theological approach to understanding the phrase "stuff happens" and conveys a heartfelt reminder that suffering is a normal part of human existence. Unfortunately, we sometimes view heartache and suffering as abnormal, as something to be fixed, cured, or solved. Because of advances in science, technology, and engineering, we've become very good at fixing, curing, and solving, so why should we suffer if there's a possible solution? The counterargument is this: Just because we're no longer threatened by saber-toothed tigers, bubonic plague, or attacking hordes doesn't mean we can escape personal pain and suffering. Often, there is no solution to human suffering. Any number of things can befall us, from big tragedies to little hassles. We hate having to wait in line, we don't like our coworker, we are stressed about family issues, or we can't stand feeling anxious and worried. We don't like how others treat us, whether it's his tone or her sarcasm. Why should we have to tolerate rude people, and why be uncomfortable or miserable, even for a little while, if we can do something about it? In short, the abiding assumption of many is that happiness is "normal" and to be expected; all else is wrong and not normal.

Indeed, pain, suffering, and negative emotional experiences are a normal part of life. These are the natural consequence of being alive in this world. In fact, we are programmed to experience negative emotions more so than positive ones. Of the six basic emotions experienced universally by humans, four are negative (anger, sadness, fear, and disgust), and only two are positive (joy and surprise, although surprises are not always positive). The dominant role of negative emotions makes sense when you consider that these emotional experiences likely kept our ancestors out of harm's way; those who ignored negative emotions such as fear were less likely to survive. Today, ignoring or running away from negative feelings won't get you killed immediately, but it is an unhealthy way to spend your life. What would change if you and your family came to see all emotions as an essential aspect of life? What would change if you as the parent developed a capacity to tolerate negative emotions, to feel your feelings, and learned to use the information contained in your emotions? How many items could you cross off your to-do list if escaping negative emotions was no longer a chief goal? What would you do with your time if you moved out of your head and into the world?

Our aim is not to dismiss the emotional suffering of individuals who face difficult life circumstances or serious psychiatric problems.

Few therapists, and certainly not us, would expect patients who suffer from a debilitating mental illness to simply suck it up and move on because a therapist saw them as "normal." In fact, for many patients, both their life circumstances and their emotional reactions are unusual and not "normal," in the sense that their capacity for managing their circumstances is constrained financially and their ability to cope is limited biologically (quicker to react, harder to soothe, slower to recover) compared with others. Where clients (*and* therapists) can be misled, however, is in how they approach the goal of emotion management. If our sole focus is to eradicate negative emotions and emotional discomfort, we will fail to recognize that healthy living is about acting wisely and in line with our values, even if we can't control what we feel.

Emotions Don't Cause Problems; Avoiding Emotions Causes Problems

The power and the prominence of negative emotions are realities of human existence, but that doesn't mean we should hunker down in an emotional bomb shelter. Psychologists who disagree on just about everything agree that persistently avoiding negative emotions is the main cause of psychological problems. That's because there's an interesting paradox here: When we try to avoid negative emotions (and unwanted thoughts), they only grow bigger and more persistent. This psychological rebound is well documented and shouldn't be ignored. Think of it this way: Ugly feelings and unpleasant thoughts are like alien creatures that gain strength when we try to control or suppress them. They feed off the energy we use trying to escape from them!

The best example of this is panic disorder, which involves recurring panic attacks. *Panic attacks* are nasty events in which our body's fight-or-flight alarm system is turned up full throttle: We sweat, our heart beats rapidly, we can't breathe, and we get

67

nauseated or dizzy. We might experience tunnel vision, our skin might tingle, or we might become convinced that we're going crazy or are going to die. For some folks, having a panic attack can lead to *panic disorder*, which is essentially the fear of having another panic attack. People with panic disorder are trying desperately to avoid any feelings that hint at panic; over time, they become really good at imagining various sensations and situations that could signal a panic attack. Any muscle twinge or chest flutter is interpreted as the start of another panic attack and the battle is on to prevent it. The good news is that most cases of panic disorder can be successfully treated in just a few sessions. The bad news is that patients have to be willing to *generate* the sensations of panic that they've been running from. With help, they can learn to live with negative feelings and sensations that might signal panic. They learn to pull back from catastrophizing thoughts about what *might* happen if they had a panic attack. In other words, they learn that a healthy response to panic is to turn toward it and to lean in.

The same is true for family problems that carry lots of emotion. Occasionally, we work with families after something really bad has happened such as a huge fight or a tragic accident. Our job is to help them face all that has happened with eyes open. These are not pleasant sessions. Family members slowly march in, barely holding up under the emotional weight of recent events. After a bit of silence, we allow everyone to get centered and be present psychologically. Then we begin with the facts. What has happened? Who was hurt? How badly? Who did the hurting? What led to the hurting? What has happened since the hurting? Was this unusual or part of a pattern?

We ask for facts but often also get opinions, especially about who's to blame or what's to be done. We try to keep opinions out of the discussion. Every few minutes, we restate the facts to be clear about what is known. When all the facts are out in the open, we offer a summary observation, a simple validation of what they've been through. We might begin by saying something like this: "This is all very sad (or tragic)" or "Wow, this is tough." We then review some of the details of what is known. There's a great deal of emotion in families telling these facts and in our restating those facts. But once we're done, breathing comes easier, tension in the room drops, and smiles are more likely. We take families "back to the scene" of things they'd like to forget, and we reconnect them to feelings they don't want to have. We have families go through this exercise because the experience carries an important lesson: Families are bigger and stronger than negative emotions. It's an important lesson. As Carl Rogers once said, "The facts are always friendly," which means we're not well served by ignoring them. With facts in hand, families can focus on and address behaviors that lead to hurtful events. They can begin working together to promote responsible behavior and healthy relationships. They can focus on the things they can control. They can learn to walk toward the barking dog.

EMOTIONS ARE SUBJECTIVE AND TEMPORARY

Emotions are a by-product of our experiences and our interpretation of those experiences. Emotions are how our mind and body first register the impact of an event. As parents, we face the daily emotions that come with providing for, living with, and caring about our children. When the events of their lives are big and scary, our emotions can be very intense: Our physiology is turned up, we think less clearly, and we might even struggle to perform the most familiar of tasks. All of this is very real, and yet the reality of our emotions, even if very intense, does not guarantee the reality of what we perceive. Emotions are subjective. That means two people can experience the same event and not feel the same way about it. There's also room for error; as parents, we could be misperceiving what has just happened. Perhaps most importantly, we could be misinterpreting the reasons for our children's behavior. Research has found strong linkages between how parents interpret child misbehavior and their use of overly harsh parenting. Parents who view child misbehavior as intentional, hostile, and openly defiant tend to be overly harsh, which increases the risk of child coercion and other misdeeds. So, when we search for information in the feelings that arise during arguments, we should remember that it is incomplete information and not proof that our children simply want to make our life difficult.

Emotions are also temporary. Emotions are not permanent conditions. Psychologists call them *states*. As humans, we move in and out of various emotional states depending on the events we encounter and our response to those events. Moving into and moving out of an emotional state are seldom deliberate acts. Emotions arrive and we must wait for emotions to fade. For some parents, it's hard to ride out the natural course of an emotional wave; instead, they prefer to escape or suppress their unpleasant emotional experiences. This is particularly true when the unpleasant emotions are anxiety, fear, or anger. Trying to avoid or escape unpleasant emotions is not a strategy that works, and it has the downside of limiting our opportunity to experience other emotions, including ones we might enjoy. Parents who don't wait for unpleasant emotions to fade or who consistently and actively avoid these feelings, have not learned that emotions fade with time. Their experience has made them wary. Missed, however, is the experience of witnessing the natural shift in our feelings over time as well as the fact that a tendency to avoid or suppress emotions keeps unpleasant emotions around longer and makes them even stronger. Indeed, parents who are extremely reluctant to experience negative emotions could risk developing a diagnosable anxiety or depressive disorder. Fortunately, these conditions can be effectively treated without medication (National Institute of Mental Health, 2022).

Admitting Fear, Sadness, and Shame Is Helpful; Venting, Fretting, and Rumination Are Less Helpful

Some emotions are said to be "withdraw" emotions: They encourage us to pull back or shut down. Examples include fear, sadness, and shame. Fear says that all is not safe and that we need to avoid potential danger. Sadness is a signal that something or someone has been lost and cannot be reclaimed. Shame is a complex emotion, blending several feelings with thoughts of self-loathing and past pain. It's what we feel when we're constantly told (by others and ourselves) that we've screwed up and don't belong. Shame is often a strongly felt prompt to be quiet, to hide, or to stay away. It's not easy to give voice to withdraw emotions. It's uncomfortable to talk about what scares us or what makes us feel sad. And shame nudges us to never show our face. Openly admitting these feelings to someone we trust means leaning into what we fear, letting go of what we lost, and conceding facts we'd prefer to forget. But when we can do that, we are made healthier by it. We move closer to *feeling well* instead of trying to *feel good*. We learn that a life *filled* with emotional experiences—positive or negative—is not a life ruled *by* emotional experiences.

Anger is a negative emotion, but unlike fear, it's an *approach emotion*. Approach emotions nudge us forward. When we're angry, we feel an urge to move toward who has slighted us or what is in our way. Sigmund Freud suggested that a cathartic release of anger— letting off steam, so to speak—is a good way to deal with anger. This idea has popular appeal, but science has shown rather convincingly that it's not helpful. In fact, it can be counterproductive. Strong venting of anger can actually make us feel angrier *and* more likely to act aggressively. It's more accurate to think of venting as practicing our show of anger and preparing to attack. There is also misinformation about anger management, which we mentioned earlier. It is commonly thought of as the ability to calm down or interrupt anger in the heat of the moment. But anger management is less about aborting anger and more about preventing the risk of an anger-driven episode. In fact, managing anger is essentially about managing the stress in our life. When we are overwhelmed by stress, our risk for an anger-driven episode is increased. It is as if we're dry kindling in a forest; it only takes a small spark to ignite an angry rant.

Another faulty strategy for managing negative emotions is fretting or worrying. Worrying is a relatively private affair, but fretting is usually noticed by those around us. Regardless of which we use, it's important to be clear about what we're doing or not doing when we worry. It helps to be alert, to plan, and to be concerned about future tasks or problems. That's putting anxiety and worry to good use and why we have that capacity. But endless worry is neither productive nor healthy; it is an ineffective way to avoid anxiety, and it offers a false sense of control. Excessive worry can feel like we're taking care of urgent business, but we're not.

A final caution is about a type of mental rewinding called *rumination*. You might have heard this term used to describe what cows do when they rechew their food. The mental version of rumination involves replaying in our mind past mistakes, old regrets, or previous losses. Rumination is adaptive *if* we can figure out what went wrong and *if* we can identify a workable solution. But some problems (e.g., death of a spouse) can't be solved, and for those prone to depression, there's a tendency to believe that *we* are the cause of our problems. In these instances, rumination is an ineffective attempt to (a) change the past or (b) absolve oneself of past mistakes. Like worry, rumination is only a brief distraction from pain, loss, shame, or regret.

MANAGING EMOTIONS AND MANAGING RELATIONSHIPS GO HAND IN HAND

Our most important, meaningful relationships (those we have with family members, close friends, and romantic partners) provide us with a mix of emotional experiences. Other things in life can also produce strong feelings—witnessing a bad wreck, listening to a favorite song, finding a mouse in our closet—but so much of what we feel day in and day out can be traced back to our relationships. The emotional output from a significant relationship can be positive or negative. When we share our life with others, we will see their struggles, we will feel their stress, and we will know their needs. When we choose to be in their lives and coordinate our life with theirs, we are likely to encounter the emotional "overhead" of being in that relationship. Sometimes their goals are not our goals, which can lead to conflict and hard questions about who gets their way. Stress and conflict raise the emotional costs of being in a relationship. Some folks don't want that overhead, so they stay out of close relationships or quickly bail when the emotional costs get too high. Responsible parents cannot and do not bail from the parent–child relationship. Responsible parents stay and face the music of parenting stress and parent–child conflict. They find ways to manage emotional overhead.

The good news for parents is that learning to manage stress and conflict is a great way to support the parent–child relationship. And there's more than one way for parents to manage stress and conflict. Some will prefer to manage stress by being problem solvers, putting time and energy into fixing whatever is causing their distress. For example, if you learn your son is having trouble in school, you might meet with his teacher, search the web for helpful information, and talk to his pediatrician about possible learning difficulties. Other parents might prefer to manage stress by attending to the emotional fallout that comes with stressful events. They might talk with friends or family members who will listen and support them, or they might take a long, hot shower to calm their mind and body. Still other parents will prefer to take a more philosophical approach to dealing with stress, looking for lessons to be learned, a silver lining, or the "true" underlying meaning of the stressful event.

Parents can also differ in how they handle interpersonal conflict. Some folks jump right into conflict, undeterred by the dangers of strong emotion, pushing ahead to "clear the air." Others avoid conflict, trusting that time will heal all wounds. There are even folks who can pull off a textbook approach to conflict resolution: They calmly state their views at the outset, they listen patiently to what others have to say, they work collaboratively to generate possible solutions, and they compromise on a plan going forward. We've read about these folks!

Because there is more than one way to manage stress or deal with conflict, it's possible that your way will not be the preferred way of your coparent or of your children. Resolving family disputes can be tricky if one parent's preferred strategy for managing stress or conflict clashes with that of other family members. You might want to fix problems on the spot, but your partner wants to spend time talking about how badly they feel. Your teen might want to hash things out and bring an end to family tension, but you might dread having a frank discussion that could lead to more conflict and more strong emotions. It's not that one way is right, and the other way is wrong. These are merely differences in style or approach. Learning to live with those differences can be a challenge, and the hardest part is recognizing that these differences exist and aren't intentional. It's only during times of stress and upheaval that we're likely to see how different members of our family deal with stress and conflict.

Our personal preference for managing stress and conflict can form rather early in life, mainly through early childhood experiences. For example, some children learn that parents are a reliable source of comfort and security and develop a willingness and capacity to trust others. Other children grow up wondering if their parent will be available when they need them most, which often leads to bigger and louder ways to alert parents about their distress; as adults, these individuals might find it hard to feel secure and close in their relationships. If parents are distant or rejecting and an unreliable source of comfort, children might learn to take matters into their own hands, no longer bothering to signal distress or even hoping for the comfort of others. When distressed, these individuals tend to pull away and isolate. Differences in how we use relationships to cope and manage stress can be carried forward into future relationships and activated during times of stress or conflict. This means we might be surprised when our mild-mannered partner reacts to stress or conflict in a way we've never seen before.

Identify Your Coping Strategies and Preferences

All parents cope with stress; some just cope better than others. Once we find a coping strategy or style that seems to work, we tend to settle into it. Researchers often group coping into various categories. The most important categories are strategies that work and strategies that don't work. A coping strategy works if it helps you endure a stressful event without much wear and tear and doesn't create additional problems. A strategy doesn't work if the stressful event basically stops you in your tracks or produces additional, significant problems. We can call these two categories *adaptive coping* and *maladaptive coping*. Another basic categorization is between active and passive coping. *Active coping* involves a direct attempt to control the stressful event or minimize its impact. *Passive coping* is usually less effective and can often involve emotional or behavioral avoidance. Here are three other ways to categorize coping:

- *Problem-focused coping* is coping designed to solve the problem that's causing stress in the first place. Here's one example: If you're stressed out because your kids haven't done their chores and the house is a mess, a problem-focused approach to coping might involve gathering everyone together and making a plan to get the chores done in a timely fashion.

Tim's View

I worked with a father who was very effective at using problem-solving skills to deal with his own stress. His wife was more emotion focused and preferred to be with loved ones, especially her husband. Usually, the difference in their coping styles was not a problem. But on one particularly stressful evening, when all seemed to be going wrong for this family, the father wanted nothing more than to be by himself while his wife wanted to be at his side! Fortunately for this couple, most of the stressful events they encountered didn't arrive at the same time. On the other hand, their daughter's growing tendency to be defiant and disrespectful forced them to re-examine how they had to work together as a team during times of stress.

- *Emotion-focused coping* is coping designed specifically to manage strong, unpleasant feelings caused by stressful events. For example, if you're freaking out because you got home and realized that chores had not been done and the house was a mess, an emotion-focused approach to coping might lead you to lie down for 10 minutes before you call everyone together and discuss your concerns.

- *Appraisal-focused coping* is coping that involves "seeing" or appraising stressful events in a more positive way. For example, a parent would be using appraisal-focused coping if they were to focus on the fact that chores weren't done because the kids were doing their homework, and that wasn't such a bad thing.

When parents can use more than one type of coping strategy, it is helpful. That's because there are times when a situation dictates a particular approach to coping. For example, some problems are rather practical or logistical in nature, and parents can solve them directly. Other problems cannot be solved, so the challenge is to manage the emotional fallout, to look for alternative meanings, or to find a positive interpretation for what's happening. For example, when a grandparent dies, parents can guide children through their feelings of grief and loss or use the occasion to discuss their family's beliefs about death and its role in the human experience.

Some parents rely on a single, preferred way of coping. For example, some people are just doers: They like to keep busy and focus on doing something or fixing whatever might be the problem. But even when the problem is not fixable, they're still fixing and doing . . . something, anything. Consider, for example, the ways people deal with the death of a loved one. Some launch into a series of tasks such as writing an obituary, helping with funeral arrangements, transporting relatives, cooking, checking on those who are struggling, and the like. It's not a bad way to cope, but it is limiting if the problem-focused copers never stop to grieve. Other parents might rely on emotion-focused or appraisal-focused forms of coping, which, again, are useful at times. We tend to prefer a coping strategy that is familiar, but that doesn't mean it's a strategy that will serve us well in all situations. Also, some forms of emotion-focused or appraisal-focused coping are clearly maladaptive. For example, overeating, abusing alcohol, smoking, impulsive shopping, and irresponsible sexual behavior can all be viewed as poorly chosen forms of emotion-focused coping. As we noted earlier, avoiding negative emotional experiences only adds to the problems in our life.

One last way to categorize different forms of coping is based on whether we cope alone or with help from others. Some parents want to be alone when feeling stressed; others want their loved ones by their side. Both interpersonal styles are useful, and neither is wrong, but one parent's style could be different from their coparent or other family members. Exhibit 3.1 illustrates the different coping options available to parents. Which option (or options) describes your typical way of coping? If you have a coparent, check to see if

EXHIBIT 3.1. Categories of Coping

Fix the problem by yourself	Feel better by yourself	Think differently by yourself
Fix the problem with others	Feel better with others	Think differently with others

you agree on your preferred method of coping. It's not uncommon for parenting partners to differ in how they cope.

Diversify Your Self-Care Portfolio

What's in your self-care portfolio? We use the term *portfolio* to describe the full set of strategies you might use for self-care and coping—all the tools you can use to benefit your health and well-being. In business, this term is used to describe your list of investments, and it can be advantageous to have a diverse portfolio. The same is true for managing our health: It can be helpful to use a diverse mix of strategies for self-care and coping. As we noted earlier, we often have a preference for using a particular type of self-care strategy, which means we tend to overlook options that are less familiar to us. For example, a father who likes to solve problems on his own might dismiss the wise counsel and emotional support offered by his spouse. Another parent might be physically fit and believe they are healthy but also feel emotionally desperate and socially isolated. If your parenting is affected by health-related concerns—emotional or physical—consider how you might diversify your self-care portfolio. Exhibit 3.2 lists options worth considering. In the first column are

---

EXHIBIT 3.2. Options for Self-Care

Skills and habits for repeated use	Tactics for occasional use
Organizational skills	Find new, supportive friends
Time-management skills	Establish a weekly date night
Deep breathing skills	Go on vacation
Assertiveness skills	Hire a babysitter
Problem-solving skills	Call a relative or old friend
Mindfulness	Join a faith community
Exercise	Simplify your schedule
Work skills	Move to a different community
Financial management skills	See your doctor for medical care
Help-seeking skills	Ask for financial assistance
Socializing skills	Find a more satisfying job
Leadership skills	Get your vision checked
Prayer or meditation	Volunteer at or give to a charity
Hobbies	Seek help from a local or govern-
Healthy sleep habits	mental agency
	Join a club
	Visit your dentist

skills and habits that can be used repeatedly to help you cope or to enhance your health and well-being. In the next column are various *tactics* that can be used once or occasionally to benefit your health and well-being. You might know of other options that you can use, either by themselves or in combination with one of these.

MINDFULNESS

One skill worth highlighting in this chapter is mindfulness. This is especially true for parents who are concerned about their emotional health and well-being. Nearly everything we've discussed in this chapter can be linked to parents' capacity for mindfulness, and scientists are learning more and more about the benefits of mindful parenting. One way to describe mindful parenting is to describe its opposite, which is mindless parenting. The word *mindless* doesn't mean stupid or dumb; it's used here to mean automatic and without deliberate thought. In fact, as we discussed in Chapter 2 on goals, much of parenting is mindless and automatic—and that's usually a good thing because it allows parents to manage multiple tasks simultaneously. The downside of automatic, mindless parenting is that some parenting habits are driven by hidden, emotion-based goals that can negatively affect our parenting and our parent–child relationships (see Chapter 2).

Before we discuss mindful parenting, let's first define it. In their 2017 book, *The Art and Science of Mindfulness*, psychologists Shauna Shapiro and Linda Carlson defined *mindfulness* as "the awareness that arises through intentionally attending in an open, caring, and discerning way" (p. 8). With this type of awareness, which is also known as *present-moment awareness*, we experience life from moment to moment without trying immediately to change that experience. Practically speaking, this is not an easy thing to do; nor is it something we can or should do all the time. Our minds are wired to focus on what's next or what has just happened. Anticipating the future and learning from the past have kept the human race alive for eons. As a result, our minds do this well and virtually nonstop. But with practice, we can add the capacity to be intentionally mindful.

The Paradox of Mindfulness

The ability to be mindful and present in the moment comes with significant health benefits—both physical and psychological. But these benefits can be elusive because mindfulness is a radically different way to use our mind, one that runs counter to our usual mental tendencies. It involves hitting the pause button on those tendencies and attending to what's here and now, without judgment and with no agenda other than experiencing and observing. Dr. Shapiro and her team (2018) described mindfulness as somewhat of a paradox, a blend of things both true and seemingly contradictory. For example, mindfulness is about acceptance *and* change: Mindfulness doesn't necessarily change what we experience in life, but it can change and deepen how we experience it. That's helpful in the face of stress and adversity because our mind's tendency is to resist the arrival and impact of adverse circumstances, which makes sense when a clear solution is available, but that's not always the case. And as Dr. Shapiro and colleagues noted, what we resist psychologically tends to persist; thus, our rush to make things different can sometimes cause prolonged suffering. We change for the better when we are first open to and accepting of what is happening in the present moment, when we insert a brief pause before we act. Other paradoxes associated with mindfulness are that it involves (a) escaping *and* engaging, (b) striving *and* nonstriving, and

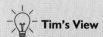

Tim's View

Pema Chödrön (1991), who has written several books on mindfulness, offered an intriguing image for those seeking to understand this paradox:

We could learn to stop when the sun goes down and when the sun comes up. We could learn to listen to the wind; we could learn to notice that it's raining or snowing or hailing or calm. We could reconnect with the weather that is ourselves, and we could realize that it's sad. The sadder it is, and the vaster it is, the more our heart opens. We can stop thinking that good practice is when it's smooth and calm, and bad practice is when it's rough and dark. If we can hold it all in our hearts, then we can make a proper cup of tea. (p. 81)

(c) focusing on the self *and* not the self. Suffice it to say that if you develop the capacity for mindfulness, you will have learned something that is quite helpful but also a bit weird, at least in the sense that it's not what we usually do with our mind.

 Tim's View

When my patients begin practicing mindfulness, I ask them to watch three short videos. All are free and on YouTube. Two are animated and very entertaining. One is on meditation and one is on mindfulness (search YouTube for "Meditation 101" and for "Why Mindfulness Is a Superpower"). The third video is a 12-minute excerpt of a talk that Jon Kabat-Zinn gave to employees at Google Corporation (search YouTube for "Mindfulness Meditation Taster with Jon Kabat-Zinn"). It is the best introduction to mindfulness I know of. Also, watching it offers a way to practice mindfulness because the video includes a 3-minute span where Kabat-Zinn has everyone quietly practicing mindfulness.

The Practice of Mindfulness

It is often said that mindfulness is simple but not easy. That has certainly been our experience as therapists. Our clients are often confused by what mindfulness is, by how to practice it, and by how to know if they're doing it "right." Our suggestion is to begin small, experimenting and playing around with this kind of *awareness-ing*, a term used by Dr. Jon Kabat-Zinn, the person primarily responsible for making mindfulness a well-known health practice. He sees mindfulness as bigger than thinking because it involves being aware of thinking. Some folks meditate to practice mindfulness, but that's not necessary or essential. Besides, the goal, at least for us and this book, isn't to help you become a meditator but to help you parent mindfully.

The practice of mindfulness is a lot like building or maintaining our body's core (the midsection with all the muscles in the front, back, and sides). When our body has a strong core, we have better posture, a healthier back, better balance, and greater ability to do various physical tasks. In a similar way, practicing mindfulness is a way to strengthen our *psychological* core, which enhances our ability to "hold" and "carry" difficult emotional experiences, to stay focused on the task at hand, to be kinder to ourselves, to be more attuned to others, and to treat others (including our children) with care and respect. Perhaps the most important thing to note is that mindfulness does *not* involve emptying the mind or stopping our thinking. That's impossible. In fact, mindfulness is not even about trying to calm the mind or relax the body, although some feel calmer after practicing mindfulness. Instead, the aim with mindfulness is simply to notice or observe what is being experienced—without judgment and without any effort to change it.

You can start practicing mindfulness right here and right now. Try this 1-minute exercise (with your eyes open or closed):

1. Whether sitting, standing, or lying down, notice and feel whatever your body is touching.
2. Mentally scan your body, starting at your feet and moving slowly to the head.
3. As you do this, notice your breath going in and out.
4. Follow an out-breath and try to notice the moment just before your in-breath.
5. Notice any thoughts you're having and then go back to your breath.
6. Follow the next out-breath. Ride it out.

If you did the exercise, how was it? Were you uncomfortable when you were trying it? How did you feel *after* trying it? Can you imagine doing this exercise 5 minutes every day for an entire month? A brief practice each day can go a long way.

Mindful Parenting

An exciting new area of study is called *mindful parenting*. Research in this area has only recently begun, but the findings to date point to important benefits when parents can take a more mindful approach to interacting with their children. For example, researchers in Vermont and Georgia (McKee et al., 2018) studied roughly 600 families to see whether parents' capacity for mindfulness or lack of mindfulness (e.g., "I find it difficult to stay focused on what's happening in the present") predicted child functioning at three developmental stages: young childhood (3–7 years), middle childhood (8–12 years), and adolescence (13–17 years). At all three stages, the research team found that higher levels of parent mindfulness predicted youth having fewer emotional problems and fewer behavioral problems. Importantly, the association between parents' capacity for mindfulness and their child's functioning seemed to operate through what the researchers called mindful parenting. Here's an example of an item assessing mindful parenting: "When I'm upset with my child, I notice how I am feeling before I take action." Mindful parenting predicted higher levels of positive parenting (e.g., "I encourage my child to talk about their troubles") and lower levels of negative parenting (e.g., "I lose my temper when my child doesn't do something I ask them to do"). However, only negative parenting was a significant predictor of children's functioning. These findings suggest that mindful parenting can lead to improvements in both positive and negative parenting but a reduction in negative parenting is more helpful. In 2021, coparents Jon and Myla Kabat-Zinn authored a paper titled, "Mindful Parenting: Perspectives on the Heart of the Matter," in which they offered this comment about mindful parenting:

> Mindful parenting is not a project to create "better" or "optimal" children (whatever that might mean), or to be "better"

84

or "optimal" parents, but to embrace in moment-to-moment awareness as best we might the entire enterprise of parenting our children in a mutuality of love and discovery and not-knowing. (p. 266)

HEALTH HOMEWORK

There's not just one way to be a healthy parent. Not everyone needs to go to the gym, lose weight, or eat oat bran to be physically healthy. Not everyone needs to see a therapist, go on retreats, or take up yoga to be emotionally healthy. You don't have to have the perfect marriage or tons of friends to have healthy relationships. And you don't have to join a church or pray to have a meaningful life and an appreciation for the transcendent. Good, healthy parents come in all forms. Do you . . . and be healthy.

1. Complete the health inventory and discuss it with someone willing to hear your health story.
2. Write a list of your preferred ways of coping and how you might diversify that list.
3. Try out a new skill or tactic that can enhance your health and well-being.
4. Practice 5 minutes of mindfulness each day for 1 month.

CHAPTER 4

STRUCTURE: THE 4 Rs OF BEING A FAMILY

Raising children is like tending to a plant, in that a child's growth and development unfold slowly over time. We must wait to see how things turn out. We can't know right away if efforts to *accept* our children helped them better manage their emotions and view themselves positively. We must wait before knowing if efforts to *contain* misbehavior have helped our children become responsible, law-abiding citizens. And when we *lead*, we can't see immediate impacts on children's core values and beliefs. In other words, the influence we have on our children is more indirect than direct. Soil, water, and sunlight do the work of nurturing plants, so the gardener's job is to ensure that these elements are available and not to over- or under-water our plants. Similarly, parents must avoid over- or under-parenting, but what are their garden plots? In our holistic, long-term model of good enough parenting, the parent–child relationship is the most important context, but other contexts also deserve parents' time and attention. Our focus in this chapter is on how parents can use structure to address the important developmental contexts of family, siblings, and peers.

This chapter aims to help you

- understand how structure relates to parenting,
- learn the 4 Rs of structure,
- establish helpful family routines,
- define key family roles,
- know when and how to use family rules,
- understand and use family rituals, and
- learn the value of holding a family meeting.

WHAT CAN STRUCTURE DO FOR YOU?

Family structure is a useful but often overlooked aspect of parenting. In families and homes that lack adequate structure, parenting is more difficult. Here are just a few reasons why structure is so helpful.

Structure Makes Parenting More Efficient

Families that are well structured have found a way to turn successful parenting practices into habits that benefit the entire family. Because so much of parenting behavior is done automatically, parents can use structure to ensure that what they do on the fly or without a lot of deliberate thought is positive and productive. Structure helps parents work efficiently, even when they're not at their best, and allows them to devote more time to self-care and to the parent–child relationship.

Structure Protects Against Stress

Stressful events can have a negative effect on children's development and disrupt parenting. For some families, the negative impact of divorce, poverty, neighborhood violence, marital conflict, or poor parent health is profound and lasting. But not all families suffer in the face of stress. In these homes, structure is used to protect and preserve parenting during times of upheaval and change. Importantly, stress is not always random, and sometimes families operate in ways that actually add stress to their lives. Families that are organized and structured tend to generate less stress.

Structure Helps Parents Manage Other, Competing Contexts

In Chapter 1, we stated that the best way to counter the influence of not-so-positive contexts in your children's lives (e.g., risky peers, unhealthy websites) is to compete and compete well and that a strong parent–child relationship is the best strategy for that competition. Now we add that how you organize your family is also quite important. Healthy families are more than a collection of isolated individuals or separate relationships; families are systems that have order, purpose, and identity. And parents can use structure to help shape their family's order, purpose, and identity.

THE 4 Rs

A convenient way to think about and remember ways to structure your home and family is the 4 Rs: Routines, Roles, Rules, and Rituals.

Routines

A family's *routine* is its daily, weekly, or monthly schedule of who does what, when, and where. Whether it's eating supper, doing homework, paying bills, folding laundry, relaxing, or getting ready for bed, your family will benefit when there's a certain degree of regularity to its routine. As family therapists, we've met a number of families whose homes are lacking in routine. Each day brings questions about if and when basic tasks will be done and by whom. Well-run families tend to have more limited periods where they lack routine (e.g., the last 2 weeks of summer when kids are finished with summer activities and just hanging out). Without the structure of a set routine, even well-run families are prone to having conflict and to hurt feelings during these unstructured times. When school starts and they reclaim their routine, things usually go back to normal.

Routines are a good indicator of family organization. In healthy, well-organized families, daily tasks (e.g., getting up, doing homework), weekend activities (e.g., grocery shopping), and monthly events (e.g., paying bills) are predictable and structured. Children generally feel safer and less anxious when they know what to expect each day. That's because children, like all humans, find chronic unpredictability to be unpleasant (even scary). Structured routines guide our behavior and give us a sense of order and predictability. A regular schedule for daily activities, such as dinnertime, bedtime, and study time, is particularly important. Compared with parents living in chaotic homes, those living in homes that have a good routine are likely to feel more settled and able to think clearer in the face of stress.

Routines should be an indicator of what's important to a family, but that's not always the case. Some families spend lots of time in activities that actually detract from family cohesion or add little to children's healthy development. Hours and hours of TV, poor planning for meals, no set time or place for homework, and unpredictable bedtimes are a few of the unwise habits families can fall into. Some families lack routine because they overcommit to activities (e.g., traveling sports teams, competitive dance squads) that require significant amounts of time and energy. Some high-functioning families can manage a busy schedule *and* lots of activities, but other families come to regret making such costly commitments.

Here's a useful exercise: Make a list of what's most important to your family. Focus on the things your family truly values and the beliefs that are most central to who you are as a family. Next, write out your family's daily, weekly, and monthly schedules. If your family doesn't really have a schedule, consider creating one; start with the things that *need* to get done and then work on building a routine from there. Compare your family's values and beliefs to what's in your daily, weekly, and monthly schedules. When examined side by side, consider whether your current family routine is a good reflection of what's important. If it's not, consider how it can be improved.

Steps to Improving Family Routines

1. **Decide if your family's routine needs changing.** If you feel disorganized—that each week brings unpredictable, high levels of stress—or your routine doesn't reflect your family's values, it might be time to change it.
2. **Begin by changing one thing at a time.** Family routines can be hard to change. Go slow and don't try to overhaul the whole schedule at once: Your family will revolt!
3. **Decide what part of your routine will have the largest ripple effect.** Here are three options you might consider: (a) the time when you eat supper, because it's often a way to start the evening and a chance for families to spend time together; (b) the total number of activities or organizations in which family members are involved; and (c) the total number of nights and hours the TV is on each week.
4. **Be realistic and don't overschedule.** Parents and children need time to transition from one activity to the next, and they need time to be alone and rest. These times can be lost when families fill their schedules with lots of activities. Some activities work much better if scheduled less frequently.

(continues)

Steps to Improving Family Routines (*Continued*)

5. **Every so often, recalibrate your routines.** Families can sometimes slip back into old, unhealthy routines. Families also need to change their routine from time to time as their needs, interests, and activities change.
6. **Have fun and be creative.** You don't have to keep the same-old schedule just because it's the way you've *always* done it. TV doesn't have to be on *every* night, some chores can be done every *other* day, evening meals don't *have* to be hot, and bath time doesn't *have* to be at night.

Roles

As a parent, you're the person in charge, the authority figure in the home. Some equate that with being the disciplinarian, but that's too narrow a perspective; there are lots of ways parents can be an authority figure, and discipline is just one of them. Healthy parents, comfortable in the role of being the authority figure, have some degree of psychological separateness from their children. They live on the other side of a firm generational boundary that differentiates them from their children. This statement might puzzle parents who find it hard to imagine being separated from their children by any kind of boundary. They might insist that it's important to have a close attachment to their children, and they wouldn't want to jeopardize the attachment relationship in any way. But the healthiest attachment bonds are derived from parenting that is sensitive and carefully attuned to children's needs, which may include times for psychological and emotional distance. In fact, *securely* attached children are comfortable being alone *and* close to others. These children are also generally better able to manage their emotions and their interpersonal relationships than children who are insecurely attached. They don't fall apart when separated from loved ones and they don't run away from intimacy. Parents who routinely intrude into children's psychological space and cross over generational boundaries are more likely to have children with an insecure sense of attachment.

To help you evaluate your family's generational boundaries, we created Worksheet 4.1. Each question asks, "Whose business is it?" You can use these questions to gauge whether you or your

WORKSHEET 4.1. How Firm Are Your Family's Boundaries?

Whose "Business" Is It?	Circle All That Apply				
Parent's hairstyle	Child	Parent	Sibling	Grandparent	Other
Child's teeth	Child	Parent	Sibling	Grandparent	Other
Monthly bills	Child	Parent	Sibling	Grandparent	Other
Parent's romance	Child	Parent	Sibling	Grandparent	Other
Child's misbehavior	Child	Parent	Sibling	Grandparent	Other
Child's schoolwork	Child	Parent	Sibling	Grandparent	Other
Child's punishment	Child	Parent	Sibling	Grandparent	Other
Parent's heartaches	Child	Parent	Sibling	Grandparent	Other
Child's room	Child	Parent	Sibling	Grandparent	Other
Child's grades	Child	Parent	Sibling	Grandparent	Other
Parent's anger	Child	Parent	Sibling	Grandparent	Other
Parent's clothes	Child	Parent	Sibling	Grandparent	Other

(continues)

WORKSHEET 4.1. How Firm Are Your Family's Boundaries? (Continued)

Whose "Business" Is It?	Circle All That Apply				
Child's friends	Child	Parent	Sibling	Grandparent	Other
Parent's work	Child	Parent	Sibling	Grandparent	Other
Children's hobbies	Child	Parent	Sibling	Grandparent	Other
Child's hairstyle	Child	Parent	Sibling	Grandparent	Other
Parent's teeth	Child	Parent	Sibling	Grandparent	Other
Child's heartaches	Child	Parent	Sibling	Grandparent	Other
Parent's friends	Child	Parent	Sibling	Grandparent	Other
Parent's room	Child	Parent	Sibling	Grandparent	Other

children are crossing generational boundaries in ways that are not healthy. We recommend filling out the worksheet and then discussing it with your coparent (if you have one) or with friends who are parents.

A firm generational boundary helps prevent the more toxic forms of parenting, those that involve role reversals or unhealthy alliances. Children can be damaged psychologically when parents use children as their primary source of emotional support. The tendency to *parentify* children is more common among parents who are emotionally immature, mentally ill, or chemically dependent. These parents *need* children to be not only loyal but also emotionally and physically available. When parentified children try to assert independence, the emotionally needy parent is likely to fall apart while also getting angry; they are scared and hurt by their children's "selfishness" and insensitivity. This kind of strong negative reaction can leave parentified children feeling guilty and confused. Over time, guilt and confusion turn to frustration and anger, which can become very intense. The most explosive and angriest children are often parentified. They've spent too many years in a damned-if-I-do, damned-if-I-don't family situation. They want independence but have little opportunity to practice it. And the cost of their independence—hurting *and* losing their parent—is simply too high.

Some parents might relax generational boundaries from time to time or take a short break from the role of authority figure, but they shouldn't do this for long. Sometimes these slips follow family disruptions such as parents' divorce. When parents are living separately, the family power structure is temporarily shaken and children can be confused about who is in charge and how far parental jurisdiction goes (e.g., mom's house, dad's house, both?). Depending on how cooperative or bitter they are, divorcing parents can make this a brief period of confusion or greatly extend it, even many years postdivorce. Especially damaging are power struggles in which children are put in the middle of divorced parents. This can involve children being asked to be loyal to only one parent, to keep secrets from the other parent, or to "spy" and "tattle" on the other parent.

In some families, there is a strong psychological alliance between a parent and a child that is stronger than the relationship between parents. This could signal long-standing marital dissatisfaction: When parents grow apart as a couple, it is fairly common to seek a stronger connection with their children, but in extreme cases with parents who are emotionally immature or psychologically unstable, this could involve "unholy alliances" that lead to bad child outcomes and possible child abuse.

Another risky scenario can be called "divide and conquer." In this situation, one parent tends to side with and "rescue" a child from negative interactions with the other parent. The rescuing parent is inclined to remove the child from the situation or chide their partner for being too harsh and out of control. Not surprisingly, the other parent feels undermined and perhaps betrayed, which only fuels resentment. That means future interactions with the child are likely to be even stormier. Of course, when that happens, the rescuing parent is now completely convinced that their partner is out of control and is damaging their child. To protect the "victimized" child, the rescuing parent tries to block any attempt by the partner at discipline for fear of it escalating. At this point, the child now has incredible power, including the power to ignore or dismiss the "angry" parent. Over time, this scenario can cause two parents who once loved each other and agreed on most aspects of parenting to morph into exaggerated caricatures of their original selves. There's the angry monster parent who is convinced the child is a manipulative little so-and-so, and there's the scared protector parent convinced that keeping their child safe means pulling away from their angry coparent.

Children who remain too long in this distorted power arrangement are at risk for learning some unhealthy habits. The worst is learning that falling apart and being overly emotional helps you escape from conflict and the unwanted demands of others. There's no learning to accept the consequences of their actions. These children are like tiny cars with huge engines: They have way more power than they can control. And once they recognize the power they have, they can use it deliberately and repeatedly to divide and conquer. Parents' tendency in this scenario is to do more of the same—either more rescuing or more attacking/demanding. One parent is working hard to prevent their partner from "hurting" their child, while their partner works hard to be the adult in the family and hold their child accountable. Both are right in a way but knowing this doesn't help. The recommended strategy is counterintuitive: Turn toward each other, rebuild the parental alliance, and re-establish a generational boundary between parents and children. Neither parent is "winning," and both want what's best for a child who is now at serious risk because of the divide-and-conquer pattern. Turning toward each other, as unpleasant as that might sound, will firm up the generational boundary and send a strong message that the parents are now working together as a team. This is the best and quickest way to correct the distortion in power and remind children of their proper role in the family.

Next, we provide 10 tips for promoting healthy boundaries and preventing unhealthy alliances. It can also help if you and your partner each draw your family's "organizational chart" and then compare them. If your children are old enough, ask them to draw one too. Who do they think is the "boss" of the family? Who is the next boss after that person? Which family members are in a team and how many teams are there? Therapists sometimes ask these outlandish questions to get family members thinking about their role in the family.

---

10 Ways to Make and Keep Boundaries in Your Family

1. Respect children's privacy and insist on them respecting your privacy.
2. Make it a rule to knock on doors before entering rooms.
3. Close (and lock) your door to maintain privacy. Allow children (older than 5 years of age) to do the same, as long as they're safe and the privilege is not abused.
4. Do not discuss issues that are inappropriate or overwhelming for children (e.g., concerns over finances or romantic partners).
5. Make necessary (possibly unpopular) decisions on behalf of the whole family.

(continues)

---

10 Ways to Make and Keep Boundaries in Your Family (*Continued*)

6. Do distinctively different things that are special with each of your children.
7. Comment on positive characteristics that set a child apart from their parents and siblings.
8. Guard well a time each day or week when you are by yourself. Announce it often.
9. Guard well a time each week or month for you and your partner to be alone together. Announce it often.
10. Guard well at least one personal hobby or interest. Announce it often.

Rules

Household rules keep life orderly when multiple people are living under one roof and sharing resources. In families, rules also help children deal with situations that are dangerous or overwhelming. Family rules are more formal than instructions because they're in effect all the time, not just when parents say them out loud. Here are some examples: "No playing in the street." "No food outside of the kitchen." "No hitting or pushing." Some rules are specific to recurring "hot spots," such as when parents are on the phone or when the family is in the grocery store. Ideally, these kinds of hot-spot rules tell children what to do in that situation (e.g., "When I'm on the phone, you should either watch TV or play in your room"). If the rule is new, it can help to have children say the rule just before or right when the situation occurs; parents can then praise children for remembering it and following it.

A FEW RULES ABOUT RULES

There are several things to keep in mind when creating and enforcing rules:

- Rules work best when used sparingly.
- Rules shouldn't be imposed hastily but only after careful observation, reflection, and planning.
- Rules should be easily understood by children and have clearly defined consequences if they do not follow them.
- Rules should be developmentally appropriate ("Keep your room clean" may be too vague for a 3-year-old but reasonable for a teenager).
- Rules should be something parents can enforce consistently (not an unrealistic expectation such as "The rule is that you two will get along and never argue with each other").

Here's an example of a poorly established rule: A mother takes her two children to the park and then gets angry when they refuse to quit playing when it's time to leave. Out of frustration, she announces her new rule: "From now on, no more trips to the park!" This rule has been set hastily, out of anger, without input from her children and is unlikely to be enforced. In addition, it was a consequence for not listening the first time, and the consequence was unclear and unpredictable for the children. This rule also doesn't solve the real problem (specifically, difficulty ending play at the park) and it will only undermine the mother's authority if and when the family goes to the park again, as her rules could be viewed as mere temporary shifts in mom's mood.

But this same scenario can be used to illustrate a more effective approach to setting rules. If the mom had stayed with her anger a bit longer, sorting out what was bothering her and taking time to consider what to do about it, she would have been more likely to recognize that her children needed help making the transition from a very fun activity to a nonplay activity. She could tell her children that she's trying to solve the *family's* problem of playtime at the park lasting too long. Framing the situation in this way fits nicely with the collaborative problem-solving model of Dr. Ross Greene (2010). In that model, child "misbehaviors" are thought to result from children lacking the skills to handle situations that are a recurring problem. When viewed this way, the goal is less about controlling children's behavior via discipline and more about equipping them with the skills or structure they need so the situation is easier to manage. Our recommendation to establish a rule is an example of the latter.

To make it collaborative, this mom can involve her children in identifying a useful rule. Depending on the age of her children, she might have them suggest rules (for older children) or she might choose a rule but ask them to comment on it (for younger children). For example, she might make a rule that says, "Mom's job at the park is to announce when there's only 5 minutes left and when there's only 1 minute left to play." The mother could then ask her children for creative ideas about how she should make these announcements ("Hey everybody! I've got five fingers in their air because we only have 5 minutes left to play!"). In this way, they can feel like it is *their* rule as well and not just "Mom's rule." Children could even give the rule a name (e.g., the Time-to-Leave Rule), further establishing it as a household fixture.

RULES FOR MANAGING SIBLING CONFLICT

If rules help parents structure situations that are potentially problematic *and* frequent, then two contexts that should benefit from family rules are those involving siblings and those involving peers. Children benefit from interacting with siblings and peers, but these interactions can also have a negative influence. *Sibling interactions* can be a problem if they involve (a) using aggression to resolve conflict or (b) the modeling of risky, problem behavior by an older sibling. *Peer interactions* can be a problem if they involve (a) lots of unsupervised time with peers who value risky, unhealthy behavior or (b) frequent opportunities for children to engage in risky, unhealthy behavior.

It is common for children to argue with siblings—a lot. Researchers who have gone into people's homes to study family life have documented this. Most sibling arguments are mild, but some sibling conflict is ugly and loud, which can escalate into physical violence. It's upsetting for parents to see children get angry and try to hurt each other. Ironically, sibling conflict is also an opportunity for children to learn valuable lessons about conflict resolution. Conflict is found in nearly every relationship, and dealing responsibly with interpersonal conflict means learning to be assertive, civil, and nonviolent. Because sibling conflict happens so often, it can be a thorn in parents' sides, *or* it can be a chance for children to learn to resolve conflict together. That will require clear rules.

The most important rule is that aggression and violence are unacceptable strategies for ending conflict. The next most important rule is that children should resolve conflict by using words spoken directly to their sibling. When children can end sibling conflict by hitting, pushing, or grabbing, they're at risk for learning that violence or the threat of violence is a powerful way to win an argument. When children are allowed to end conflict by complaining to a parent who rescues them, they are at risk for learning that others will do their talking for them and there's no need to be assertive. In both scenarios, the chance to learn how to speak directly and to act nonaggressively is lost.

Sometimes parents feel caught between two different strategies when it comes to sibling conflict. One is a hands-off approach in which parents allow siblings to use whatever means possible, including physical fighting, to end conflict. The dangers of this strategy should be obvious: Children could learn that aggression works. When used repeatedly over time, this could even set the stage for one sibling abusing the other. One small advantage to this approach is that when children are given free rein in how to settle their conflict, a stable pecking order often emerges, which generally leads to less overall conflict. Of course, this means that one sibling is likely stuck in a submissive role; unfortunately, this could lead to negative consequences for the child such as low self-esteem, difficulties with being assertive, and feeling alienated from the family. A more commonly used strategy is for parents to intervene at the first sign of any sibling dispute. With this approach, the unpleasantness of sibling conflict is quickly halted, children aren't allowed to be bullies, and children are protected from hurtful siblings. The downside is that there are few opportunities for children to practice conflict resolution and parents will be pulled into lots of conflicts.

An intermediate approach begins with intervening whenever conflict involves physical violence, but coaching children through conflict resolution. This prevents unintended lessons about the value of using aggression, it protects children from abuse by a sibling, and it allows children to learn to resolve conflict on their own. Guidelines for being a conflict coach are summarized next.

Coaching Children Through Sibling Conflict

Set Primary Goals

- Help children learn to resolve conflict on their own without violence.
- Manage the noise of sibling conflict separately from the resolution of conflict.

Create Advanced Goals

- Once children are better at communicating, help them resolve conflict through taking turns and compromising.

Coaching Children Through Sibling Conflict (*Continued*)

Identify When to Stop Sibling Conflict

There are only two reasons for parents to stop sibling conflict:

1. physical violence (hitting, grabbing, breaking things) and
2. teaming up (two or more children against one).

If There Is Violence

Impose a sanction (e.g., loss of privileges; see Chapter 6) whenever you have clear evidence of children using violence.

If There Is Teaming Up

Remind your children about not teaming up. Remind them the only *teams* in the family are the parent team and the children team.

If the Conflict Is Only Noise (Loud Arguing but No Violence and No Teaming Up)

Allow children to resolve conflict on their own, using their words. You can deal with the noise by

- going to another room or putting on headphones,
- telling children to move to another room or to a designated "arguing spot," or
- telling children to lower their voices.

If a Child Tattles, It's Time to Coach

When children tattle, give them words and behaviors they can use to settle conflict on their own—without violence. Here are some examples:

- "Ishan, tell your sister that she's being mean, and that you don't like it. Look directly at her and say it clearly and slowly."
- "Debra, I know you get mad when Robert takes your stuff, but I can't let you hit him. We don't hurt each other in this family. If you're mad, use these words: 'Robert, I don't like it when you take my stuff. I want you to stop it.'"

These guidelines can help children feel safe and supported as they learn the skills of effectively resolving interpersonal conflict. Coaching children safely through sibling conflict requires a strict limit on the use of violence. Once that foundation is in place, there should be few instances where parents must intervene. However, that will mean separating the "noise" of conflict from the resolution of conflict. In fact, it's often the loud, emotional messiness of sibling conflict that compels parents to intervene. To address this part of the conflict, children can be told to lower their voice, to take their argument outside, or to go into another room. Parents are also free to seek their own quiet solitude away from the noise of the conflict. A message to lower the noise of conflict can be as simple as, "Hey, guys. Lower your voices. Thanks." Over time and with the practice opportunities you provide, children can learn more advanced, less noisy ways to settle interpersonal disputes (e.g., taking turns, compromise).

It's more helpful for parents to be a conflict *coach* than a conflict *referee*, and this is especially true when children tattle on their siblings. That's usually a sign they need help learning to speak directly to their sibling. Think of it as a football player going to the sideline to get the next play from the coach; the coach offers guidance but stays on the sideline. In a similar way, parents can guide children who tend to complain about their siblings but avoid speaking directly to them. Consider a situation in which a boy is complaining to his father that his older sister is cheating at a game they're playing. Being a conflict coach in this instance does *not* involve the boy delivering a message *from* his father; instead, the aim is to coach the boy to deliver *his own* message. For example, the dad might say, "I'm sorry your sister isn't playing fair. Use these words the next time that happens: 'I don't like it when you cheat. It's not fair. I want you to stop.'" Notice how the dad uses this event to provide his son with a basic lesson in how to be assertive.

He's modeling the use of *I* statements and a specific script (I don't like it when you _____. It makes me feel _____. I want you to _____.) shown to help children manage conflict in positive ways. Thus, tattling has been transformed into an opportunity for his son to learn a valuable lesson in resolving conflict, and because his coaching is happening in real time, the lesson is that much more meaningful.

Rules for Managing Peer Influence

Children's interactions with peers, including friends and dating partners, can have a substantial effect on their development. Some parents downplay the influence of peers, and others view peer pressure as a serious threat to their children. Some parents forget that the impact of peer pressure can be positive or negative (or both). Reaping the benefits of positive peer pressure is more likely when children are involved with prosocial peers and positive youth activities. When children can't access those kinds of peers or peer activities, parents must look to their community for opportunities that offer positive youth development activities. Examples include Boys and Girls Clubs, Big Brothers Big Sisters, sports teams, and performing arts groups.

It's also worth noting that negative "peer" influence can happen right in your own home. We're referring to the cool, older sibling who is defiant and disrespectful toward their parents, ignores family rules, and engages in assorted deviant activities but is looked up to by younger siblings. This is a particularly hazardous situation for parents because it's tough for parents to compete with an older sibling who is seen as powerful, appealing, and cool. Wise parents don't ignore the compelling nature of this in-home example of bad behavior. If it persists for even a short time, younger siblings could start to emulate it. It can help to acknowledge that this is happening while also framing that the older sibling's behavior is at odds with what the family believes and values.

A strong parent–child relationship and a healthy family system are helpful tools when competing against the temptation of peer pressure. Parents can err if they wage too strong a campaign against peers and peer activities. It could undermine the good work parents have done to promote a solid relationship with their son or daughter. But it's also naive to think that your relationship with your children or their ties to the family will protect them from all negative peer influence. Even children who love and respect their parents can benefit when parents monitor and structure their children's peer activities. There's also value in limiting children's access to risky peer-related activities. Many parents wisely prohibit preteens and younger teens from dating, from going to friends' houses if no parents are there, or from going anywhere with friends they don't know. When children become teenagers, there are additional family rules to consider. Here are a few examples:

- No driving with more than one passenger.
- No riding with inexperienced or intoxicated drivers.
- No one-on-one dates with someone unknown to parents.
- No going to homes where alcohol is served to minors.

These rules can help but not guarantee that your children will be protected from the negative influence of peers. In fact, it can be hard sometimes to know exactly what children and their friends are doing. That's why it's important to closely track children's peer interactions and supervise them when possible. Parents will find it difficult to establish rules about peer involvement if all they know is based on fear or conjecture. Research is clear that youth who associate with deviant peers engage in more misbehavior, but is that because kids who misbehave influence other kids or is it because kids who misbehave select friends who also misbehave? Scientists find support for both hypotheses. Scientists also find that when parents know little about their children's peer-related activities, children are more likely to be more involved in deviant behavior. Is that because children are more likely to misbehave when parents don't adequately supervise them or is it because children who frequently misbehave are less likely to tell parents what they're doing or where they're going? Once again, there is scientific support for both hypotheses.

What can parents do if their children don't want them knowing where they are, who they're with, or what they're doing? Should parents simply trust their children? How much freedom should parents give them? We can't be witness to all that our children hear, see, and do. We won't always know when they're offered beer, cigarettes, or drugs. We won't always know if they've been tempted to have sex. This lack of knowing can be frightening. Some parents find solace in the belief that years of good parenting can prepare their children to make wise choices—on their own. And research supports this notion, especially if the parent–child relationship is solid and children feel connected to and heard by their parents. But if parents really want to know more about their children's peer-related activities, they'll likely have to spend time interacting with their children and their children's friends. That could mean opening your home to small hordes of kids who play video games, eat everything in sight, and sometimes damage the furniture. It could also mean getting to know the parents of those other kids. Don't be shy about chatting with the parent of your child's best friend. Remember, it takes a village.

Consider also setting rules about keeping parents informed about time spent with friends, about getting to know their friends, and about getting to know their friends' parents. Have a rule that new dating partners will be subject to careful but cordial scrutiny.

Have a rule about computers in a common area and be transparent about it: Explain that this makes it easier for you to monitor what they're doing on the computer. No one is fooled and no one gains when parents try to sneak around to gather information about their children's activities with friends and peers. Be as open and transparent as you can be ("I know you don't like this rule, but I read somewhere that it's a good idea"). With teenagers, it's useful to have a weekly activity that helps you stay informed. The best activities are fun and give your teen a reason to spend time with you (e.g., going to their favorite fast-food place). Consider having your teen invite a friend, which can make the activity fun for everyone and increase the odds that you learn new things about your child. The goal is to be an engaged, curious, but nonintrusive presence in their lives, ready to learn about them when given the opportunity.

Rituals

Rituals are the punctuation marks of life. Rituals mark occasions, signal transitions, help us manage strong emotions that come with big events, and remind us of what's truly important. Nearly all rituals—birthdays, graduations, weddings, funerals—come with scripts that guide us through these important and often emotional events. But rituals can also be used to promote a child's sense of acceptance or belonging. If rules are "standing orders" for how children should behave, then rituals are "standing invitations" for children to be a part of the family. Some parents have trouble delivering a consistent message of acceptance. Perhaps they're not very warm or maybe their children are rather uncooperative. Perhaps there are significant life stressors (money issues, work problems, family illness) that get in the way of delivering a message of acceptance. Rituals are a handy way to strengthen the parent–child relationship and make children feel loved, even when parents aren't feeling very loving.

MINIRITUALS AND MAJOR RITUALS

Family rituals don't have to be grand or elaborate to be useful. Some families embed simple rituals into their daily or weekly routine. Dinnertime, bedtime, car rides, and trips to the grocery store are all opportunities for a *miniritual* that makes the activity just a bit more fun and special. Examples include giving two hugs and a kiss each day before children get on the school bus, drawing doodles on children's lunch bag, or reading a book before bed. It's generally easier to establish rituals when children are younger, but even teenagers can get into the spirit of a fun family ritual. A good example of a miniritual is dinner time. Some families use dinner as a time when everyone takes a turn saying how their day went or how their week is going. Some families share high points and low points in their day. Other families take turns giving thanks before the meal. Of course, it can often be a challenge to find a time when everyone can sit together for a meal. If that's the case, then the ritual can be the reason for the family to gather. Examples include a make-your-own-pizza night, family movie night, fast-food night, or family game night.

Research Highlight

Studies have shown that families who eat dinner together have children who do better academically, have lower rates of depression and anxiety, use substances less, have a lower risk for teen pregnancy, and enjoy higher levels of self-esteem and resiliency. There is also evidence that for families in which a parent has alcoholism, maintaining family rituals can reduce the likelihood that their children will be problem drinkers (Wolin et al., 1988).

Ironically, one of the most valuable family rituals doesn't involve children, at least not directly. We're referring to regular, predictable opportunities for parents to take a short break from the responsibility and emotional weight of parenting. In our experience, this kind of miniritual can benefit the entire family. It's a reliable way to enhance parents' health and well-being, it's an effective strategy for maintaining a firm generational boundary, and it can be built into a family's weekly or monthly routine. Simply knowing there is a regularly scheduled break from the job of parenting can be a huge lift for parents' morale. When parents can take advantage of brief, scheduled breaks from parenting, they reduce the risk of burnout and create a reliable way to renew their energy, strength, and commitment. And by regularly and briefly separating from their children, parents send a clear message about their role as the leader of the family and about the importance of their own health and well-being.

Unfortunately, this incredible gift to family functioning is often overlooked by parents who view it as unnecessary or inaccessible. Some parents wait until they're at the end of their rope before taking a break from parenting; others wait for a longer, special break, such as a vacation trip planned the following year. Parents who don't take short (1–3 hours), regularly scheduled breaks from parenting are less likely to know and appreciate their incredible value. The real value of these breaks is not as a solution for parenting burnout but as a tool for preventing parenting burnout. Parents who take brief, regular breaks aren't waiting for their "tank" to run empty before they stop and refuel.

To be fair, some parents would gladly welcome regular breaks but find that such breaks are difficult to do logistically or financially. The obstacles can be real, significant, and numerous. Examples include the need for child care, the cost of doing whatever is planned (e.g., dinner), and the challenge of finding a workable day and time for a break. As therapists, we brainstorm with parents about brief, no-cost or low-cost ways they can take a break from parenting. Some parents join a parenting "co-op," in which parents share child care responsibilities with other parents they come to know and trust. No- or low-cost options for parenting breaks include calling a friend, sitting quietly with a book, or taking a walk in the park. Other barriers are more emotional and include feeling guilty about briefly separating from children or worrying that children won't be safe if left in someone else's care. If parents can work around these obstacles and put on their schedule (every week or month) a short break from parenting, they will have created a rich resource that can serve them well for years.

Major rituals take families out of their routine and are meant to be special. Major rituals are less frequent and more formal than minirituals and are typically used to mark important transitions or accomplishments. Birthdays, weddings, funerals, and graduations are common occasions for major rituals, as are religious and secular holidays and family reunions. These events often bring strong emotions and a bit of uncertainty about what will happen during the event or what it could mean for the future of the family. Major rituals usually have a pattern or script that participants are expected to follow, and these scripts help guide us through all the feelings that often come with major rituals. For example, the joy of seeing one's child get married is often a mix of anxiety about how to act during the ceremony, joy for the love being shared, and fear for the child's future. Parents might also feel sad or nostalgic when they see their child is grown and on their own path. Fortunately, wedding ceremonies, like other major rituals, come with shared knowledge and expectations about everyone's role, which helps us get through them while feeling all the feels.

Starting or Tweaking a Family Ritual

Some families have rituals that serve them well and should be treasured and preserved. In other families, rituals are lacking or don't

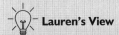

Lauren's View

Take a moment to list all of the minirituals in your family. Ask others in your family to check your list. If you are hoping to make new rituals, come up with some ideas with your child (this process can help increase buy-in from a teen). Then make a list of major rituals your family does. Consider for each of these rituals what has worked and if there are things that haven't worked. How well do your family rituals promote feelings of acceptance and connection? Focus on ways to make them more enjoyable and sustainable.

work well. Changing or creating a family ritual can take a bit of planning and creativity (or creative borrowing). We find that families are happy to talk about their favorite rituals, so consider asking around to get some ideas that might work for your family. Important to the success of a family ritual is whether it helps children feel valued and families feel like a family. Parents should keep these goals in mind when planning a new ritual. For example, if your family likes to celebrate birthdays, think of activities that help convey to the birthday person a heartfelt message of love and belonging. This could mean a personalized handwritten note, their favorite kind of cake, or a special loving toast during a birthday meal.

Some family rituals are elaborate affairs that cost lots of time and money but fail to provide children with a message of acceptance or families with a sense of cohesion. In fact, it is not uncommon for parents to be irritable and weary after all their planning and preparation. When this happens, some of the joy that comes with these special moments is lost. In fact, it's not unusual for major rituals to leave some family members regretting they ever participated. Tapping into the potential of a family ritual will require some planning as well as a certain willingness to take a risk and try something new. This shouldn't be a problem if parents are comfortable in the role of family leader, but other parents might balk at starting a new ritual because they fear pushback.

For example, every year in the United States, large amounts of food are prepared, and homes are opened to visiting family and friends to celebrate Thanksgiving. What makes for a "successful" Thanksgiving holiday? Some might point to the quality or quantity of food they eat, but we suspect most would say it's a chance (a) to give thanks for what they have and (b) to visit with friends and family members. If that's true, then the next question is how much time should be devoted to these important aspects of Thanksgiving?

We suspect that in many homes very little planning is done on these fronts. Compare that with the amount of time spent preparing food and drink. As a result, what commonly happens is that visitors are greeted, all eat their fill, some drink too much, and then everyone leaves. Of course, some families consider Thanksgiving a success when no one gets hurt and the police aren't called! But what if giving thanks and reconnecting with others were the top priorities of the day? How would that change the look and structure of Thanksgiving gatherings? Lots of families have creative, memorable traditions that are part of every Thanksgiving: an annual football game, a daylong jigsaw puzzle, a potluck dinner with everyone's favorite dish, or a long family walk after dinner. Some families pay special attention to giving thanks before everyone dives into the turkey. In some families, everyone—adults and children—is invited to say what they're thankful for. Some families literally break bread together, passing around a piece of bread from which each person pulls a small bit while giving thanks.

Here is a list of suggestions you can use when changing or creating family rituals. Consider your own rituals or finding new ones to prioritize for your family.

DIY Guide to Family Rituals

- Rituals are an opportunity for children to feel accepted by parents and for families to feel like a family.
- Rituals are (a) special ways that families do ordinary things (like mealtime or bedtime) or (b) special ways to mark events that only happen once a year or less (like graduations or weddings).
- Changing a family ritual or starting a new ritual can feel strange, but it can also be fun. Try a new ritual before you decide to keep it.
- Talk with other families about their rituals and borrow what you like.
- *Any* ritual, no matter how small, can be a success if the tone or the mood is warm and pleasant. As the parent, it's your job to set that tone. How family members treat each other during a ritual is *the* most important activity.
- *Any* ritual, no matter how big or fancy, can be a failure if the mood is cold or hostile. Don't work too hard on a major ritual if it's going to feel to everyone like a major disaster. It's better to keep it small, meaningful, and positive.
- Don't start too many rituals. The best rituals fit your schedule and are not too hard to maintain.
- Keep these questions in mind when changing or creating a family ritual:
  - What's the focus or activity of this ritual (e.g., bedtime, birthdays, making and eating tacos)?
  - Who does what and when in this ritual?
  - How often will this ritual occur (e.g., daily, weekly, monthly, yearly)?
  - Is there a name for this ritual?
  - What part of this ritual promotes acceptance?
  - What part of this ritual promotes family cohesion?
  - What can I do or say to make this ritual special and positive?
  - What do I want this ritual to mean to my child and to my family?

FAMILY MEETINGS

One kind of family ritual that is seldom used but especially helpful is the *family meeting*. Not all families have meetings, but nearly all families can benefit from them. As family therapists, we've coached parents through their first family meeting, often conducted while we were present in a therapy session. Organizing and leading a family meeting can make some parents feel uncomfortable. It means being front and center as the leader of the family. However, it's not a time for parents to be bossy. Well-run meetings engage everyone attending, seek everyone's input, and produce an outcome that all can endorse. Family meetings are particularly useful when the stakes are high, such as planning a family vacation, discussing a move to a new home or a different community, sharing news about parents' new job or work schedule, or broaching with children that parents are planning to separate or divorce. In some ways, the purpose of the family meeting is less important than the meeting itself. Imagine calling a family meeting, greeting everyone at the start, sharing your reason for the meeting, asking everyone for input, and then ending with a shared decision about next steps. What would it mean for your family if you were to run such a meeting, where all felt heard and invested in the outcome? We suggest it would feel like a family!

Family Meetings

- Decide on the main goal of the meeting (keep it small).
- Decide how much time is needed and schedule accordingly.
- Create a positive atmosphere (e.g., snacks, sodas).
- Set the ground rules for communicating, including for talking (How long? How do you know who has the floor?) and listening (No interrupting. Take turns. Parent follows with a summary).
- Follow these problem-solving steps:
  - Define the problem.
  - Generate solutions (brainstorming).
  - Evaluate the possible solutions.
  - Choose one solution to try.
  - Decide how your family will determine whether the solution worked.

STRUCTURE HOMEWORK

A family's structure is the way its members live together and how they relate to each other and to those outside the home. In this chapter, we discussed how the 4 Rs—Routines, Roles, Rules, and Rituals—make parenting efficient and serve to buffer parenting against stress and upheaval.

- Take time to review the handouts and guidelines included in this chapter.
- Think carefully about ways to establish more effective Routines, Roles, Rules, and Rituals in your family.
- Practice scheduling and running a family meeting.

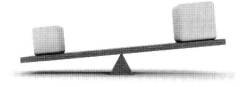

CHAPTER 5

ACCEPT: LESS IS MORE

Our holistic, long-term model of parenting combines aspects that support and are *foundational* to the parent–child relationship—Goals, Health, and Structure—with features that are *essential* to that relationship being healthy and strong. The three essential "ingredients" are parents' capacity to Accept, Contain, and Lead. We address each separately, but it's important to keep in mind that these three converge into a single whole—a parent–child relationship capable of shepherding your child to become a healthy, productive adult.

Parents need a practical and sustainable way to combine all three relationship conditions. There's a tendency when parenting children who

 Tim's View

I grew up in south Louisiana, where there are two uses for the term "holy trinity." One is the kind you learn in Catholic grade school. The other is the nickname for celery, onions, and bell pepper—three ingredients added to a roux when cooking gumbo or any other Cajun dish. Offered here is yet another version of the holy trinity—three essential ingredients that make up a healthy parent–child relationship: Accept, Contain, and Lead.

can be difficult or strong willed to move back and forth between overly strict discipline and broad permissiveness, as parents try the former but then give up and shift to the latter when fatigued or frustrated. Neither approach is particularly helpful. The good news is that parents who can accept, contain, *and* lead create a healthier and more adaptive path for their child's growth and development. So, let's first learn about acceptance.

This chapter aims to help you

- learn what it means to be accepting of your children,
- learn why that's important, and
- learn how to adopt a posture of acceptance.

THE DEFAULT MODE OF PARENTING

To *accept* is to convey a message of belonging. When put into words, the message might sound like this: "You are my child and a part of this family. What you think, what you feel, and what you do won't change that." Although they are related, accepting is not the same thing as loving your child. The key difference is that love is much grander and multifaceted. Everything you do for your children is done because you love them: setting rules, feeding them breakfast, grounding them, checking on their grades, or taking them to the doctor. All of these are ways you show your love for your children. We know that and you know that, but children can't easily see and know that. So, parents also need to show acceptance—intentionally, sincerely, and repeatedly.

What does it mean for children to be accepted? We'll answer this question with a question: What's it like to be your child? Do you find that your children are open about their feelings? Do they share their thoughts with you? Do they seem relaxed and comfortable around you, or do they seem cautious or reluctant to say much? Do they feel the need to pause and look over their shoulder to see if what they're about to say or do is okay with you? Children who feel accepted are more likely to share their thoughts, opinions, and emotions with their parents. They are comfortable in their skin and feel free to be their true selves around you and others. Of course, some children are naturally shy and inhibited, and they may be unlikely to share much of themselves even when they do feel safe and accepted. For such children, it's useful to think in relative terms—how accepted they feel with their parents compared with other adults.

What does it mean for parents to be accepting? It can mean at least three things. First, it means taking the time and making the effort to get to know children as they truly are. Second, it means believing in, loving on, and valuing the whole child—personality, feelings, quirks, passions, dreams, talents, limitations, annoying tendencies, fears, and so on. It's not being picky about the parts you accept. Third, it means delivering a consistent message of belonging and a persistent effort to understand. In this way, children have little doubt about where they stand with you. Ideally, accepting will become your default mode of parenting, what you'll use routinely, most of the time, when you're not doing a specific task such as feeding, fixing, or fussing.

A message of belonging is best delivered sincerely and consistently. What does it look like? If you thought, "Lots of listening?" you'd be spot-on. Parents are often busy people managing several tasks, so turning toward children, focusing on them and them alone, and simply being *with* them, even for a short time, can be challenging. But it doesn't need to be big or elaborate. In fact, a key feature of accepting is that *less is more*. In fact, going small and moving slowly in your effort to be accepting can make it even more powerful. To help you understand this rather elusive concept of acceptance, we offer the following fable. It's corny but illustrates nicely what it means to operate from a position of acceptance.

The Story of Little Raccoon and Standing Tree

Standing Tree heard Roxie, the little raccoon, crying long before she saw her. It was a sad, woeful lament, one that tugged at Standing Tree's roots, roots buried deep beneath the earth. She was also surprised at how small Roxie was, way too small to be carrying such sadness, she thought.

"Little raccoon," Standing Tree said gently, "you're very small, yet so very sad."

Roxie looked up at the towering tree and said, "I *am* sad, for I have no mother. She was killed by the Grey Wolf that lives in the next forest."

Standing Tree's heart went out to Roxie. She felt the weight of her grief and said, "You are so young and so very sad because you have no mother. Now I know why you were crying."

"I'm sorry. Was I too loud? I'll move on if my crying bothers you."

"No need to leave, little one," said Standing Tree in her softest voice. "Crying is what you do when your heart is broken. Besides, I'm a tall oak who has lived through many troubles; I understand sadness and crying. So, take your time. I'll be here if you need me."

Roxie cried for a very long time and then fell asleep, curled up next to Standing Tree.

The next morning, Roxie awoke and saw Standing Tree close by, just as she had promised.

Roxie looked up and said, "Hi. I didn't tell you my name. It's Roxie."

"Hi, I'm Standing Tree."

"Thanks for letting me stay. I get lonely and scared without my mother. I wish she were here."

"You miss her, and you wish she were here with you now, so you wouldn't feel scared and alone."

"That's right," said Roxie. "If she were here, we'd run and climb and fish for minnows. And she would hold me, and she'd tell me everything is okay."

"Yes, that's what mothers do. I'm sorry your mother is gone. What will you do now?"

"I hope to find a new mother, someone who can do all the things my mother did. Then I won't ever feel lonely or sad or scared."

The Story of Little Raccoon and Standing Tree (*Continued*)

Standing Tree said nothing. She looked wistfully into Roxie's eyes and could tell the little raccoon was thinking.

Suddenly Roxie announced, "I think I'll ask Brown Bear to be my mother. She lives in a nice warm cave, and she has plenty of sweet honey."

Standing Tree wished Roxie well and watched as she headed off to find Brown Bear.

When she arrived at Brown Bear's cave, Roxie leaned in and offered her greetings. Brown Bear invited her in, saying, "I know you. You're Roxie, the little raccoon who lost her mother."

"That's right," said Roxie. "May I please live here with you?"

Brown Bear was a caring creature who quickly replied, "But of course you can live here. My cave is safe and warm, and I have plenty of honey. We can be safe and warm together, and you will never have to be sad again."

Roxie did feel safe and warm in Brown Bear's cave. But Brown Bear was also very protective. Each day she warned Roxie of the Grey Wolf, the hungry Lion, and the dangerous river, saying, "You never know what might happen. Stay here with me. You can be safe, and you'll never feel sad or lonely or scared again."

Roxie appreciated Brown Bear's kindness but felt she couldn't stay. She wasn't sure where she was going the next morning when she sneaked out of Brown Bear's cave, but she walked on and on, lost in her sadness and wishing for her mother. She was soon at the spot where she had met Standing Tree. She smiled, recalling how the towering oak had said it was okay if Roxie felt sad or cried.

"Hi, it's me, Roxie!"

"Well so it is. Hi, Roxie! How is Brown Bear?"

"She's very nice and she kept me safe and fed me sweet honey, but . . . I don't know . . . I want to run and climb and fish for minnows. I think I need a different mother."

"I'm sorry things didn't work out. What will you do now?" inquired Standing Tree softly.

(continues)

> **The Story of Little Raccoon and Standing Tree (*Continued*)**
>
> Roxie thought for a while and said, "I like playing by the river. I think I'll ask Busy Beaver to be my mother."
>
> Standing Tree hoped the little raccoon would find what she was looking for. She wished her well and watched her march excitedly toward the river and Busy Beaver's home.
>
> Busy Beaver welcomed Roxie, saying excitedly, "It would be great to have you here. The more the merrier, I say! In fact, you can start right away by helping build our dam."
>
> Roxie loved being outdoors and enjoyed learning how to gather twigs and branches. She took pride in helping to build the dam, which was now quite large. Indeed, Roxie wondered when they might have time to play.
>
> She approached Busy Beaver and asked, "Is the dam big enough for us to take a holiday?"
>
> Busy Beaver chuckled and said, "Poor girl. There's too much work to be done. We'll never have the biggest dam on the river if we spend our time playing."
>
> Early the next morning, Roxie slipped out of the beaver den and headed for the spot where she knew she'd find Standing Tree. Roxie felt drawn somehow to the foot of the comforting oak.
>
> Standing Tree gazed sweetly at the little raccoon and slowly lowered her branches, just enough to let Roxie know that she was safe and welcome. Standing Tree remained silent and smiled. Roxie let go a heavy sigh and lay down beside her.
>
> Neither spoke for a very long time. It was quiet and peaceful and felt right to Roxie. She had finally found her new mother.

This short fable illustrates a distinct way to interact with a child. A central theme in the fable was Standing Tree's ability to remain still and accepting even when discussing those aspects of Roxie's situation that were unpleasant or could lead most adults to fix or help. Standing Tree stayed present in a way that conveyed acceptance while also maintaining a certain level of respect and distance, emotionally and psychologically. The image of a tree helps to emphasize that less is more when it comes to parental acceptance. Our hope is that this short fable will help you appreciate that fundamental aspect.

LEARNING TO ACCEPT

Some ways that parents convey acceptance are easy to learn and relatively easy to do; others are more complicated. But *all* can be learned, if practiced. The following sections detail the important features of simple versus more complicated forms of parental acceptance and provide examples of each.

Simple Forms of Accepting

Simple ways to convey a message of belonging to your children include being still and quiet, listening and following, using facial expressions, describing what you see, and parroting or paraphrasing. We describe each next.

BE STILL AND BE QUIET

As odd as it seems, the simplest way to convey a message of belonging is to do very little. If you're a parent heavily invested in your child's care and management, it can be hard to turn down the intensity of your parenting. Very active parenting can

 Tim's View

My patients hear me say, "We are what we practice." It's a reminder that psychological difficulties are often the result of *practicing* behaviors that don't serve us well (e.g., avoiding or suppressing our feelings). It's also a reminder that the benefits of therapy come from learning and *practicing* new, different, and more adaptive ways to behave. For some, that's like learning to play a musical instrument or learning a new language; it will require repeated practice over time.

Lauren's View

When I'm complaining about something, say an embarrassing misunderstanding or some annoying policy at my bank, friends and loved ones will sometimes respond with comments like "Did you try this?" or "Why didn't you do that?" Their immediate response to *fix* my problem can come from a good place but actually make me feel more frustrated. Sometimes I just want to have someone listen and understand. I'm quite capable of adjusting, adapting, and apologizing, but I need to feel *heard* before I move on. This can also be true for our children. Similarly, when we are truly present and open to hearing our children, we empower them and provide a safe "space" for them to share their thoughts and feelings. Don't underestimate the power of being quiet and simply listening. Remember, less is more.

make you feel better, but for children, it can sometimes be limiting or even invalidating. A useful alternative is simply to be still and quiet. It might look like you're doing nothing, but inside, it won't feel like nothing. And your quiet presence certainly won't be nothing to your son or daughter. Indeed, your children might want an explanation if they're not accustomed to having you spend time with them. It's easy to make it less weird. You could look at a magazine as you sit nearby, or you could confess to being curious about them: "I just want to spend some time with you. Maybe I'll learn something I don't know, like why you like this TV show."

LISTEN AND FOLLOW

The next option involves a more open message of belonging. It involves listening to and following your child—moment to moment—tracking what's said or done and what your child might be thinking or feeling. With this option, you're more fully investing in this moment with your child. And by joining with children, in their world, parents learn about and come to appreciate children as they are. There's simply no better way to convey a message of acceptance to children than by spending time listening and following along.

USE FACIAL EXPRESSIONS

There are lots of ways to enhance the time you set aside for listening to and following your children. One way to show that you're paying attention and tracking what they're doing and saying is through your facial expressions. Try to match emotionally what is happening or what they're saying. This requires putting down your phone or stopping whatever you're doing and looking at your child as they speak. The rest requires you to just listen and try to empathize with how they feel.

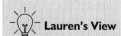 **Lauren's View**

It can be confusing when children are upset over things that we don't think should bother them. But we should be careful when trying to explain or make sense of children's emotions. We help them more when we work to understand *what* they feel and not *why* they feel.

DESCRIBE WHAT YOU SEE

Another strategy is to describe what you see your child doing. It's like being the play-by-play announcer at a ball game: You simply describe what you see as it's happening. In this way, children know that you're really paying attention. Here are some examples:

- "You're using the pink crayon to color your dragon."
- "Looks like you're doing fractions for math homework."
- "You must really like this show! You are laughing so hard."

PARROTING OR PARAPHRASING

You can also show acceptance by listening and repeating verbatim what your child is saying (parroting). Parroting is one of the skills used in *reflective listening*, a basic tool for relationship building. The listening is "reflective" in that you're like a mirror, reflecting back what your child just said. This is helpful because children might doubt if you're really listening to what they're saying, but there will be little doubt if they hear their words parroted back to them. Here's an example:

> *Child:* School sucks. And Mr. Pinkerton is a jerk. Why did I have to get him for a teacher?
> *You:* School sucks and Mr. Pinkerton is a jerk. Why *did* you have to get him for a teacher?

Play-by-play announcing and parroting will seem odd and mechanical at first, but over time your children will come to appreciate your efforts to listen and get to know them. You can make it less odd by repeating only part of what was said. Here are examples:

> *Child:* School sucks. And Mr. Pinkerton is a jerk. Why did I have to get him for a teacher?
> *You:* School sucks. *or*
> Mr. Pinkerton *is* a jerk. *or*
> Why *did* you have to get him for a teacher?

An even better way to avoid the oddness of parroting is to *paraphrase* what your child says. So rather than repeat your child verbatim, use your own words to say back what you heard (or thought you heard). Here's an example:

Child: School sucks. And Mr. Pinkerton is a jerk. Why did I have to get him for a teacher?

You: You hate school, and you wish you were never put in Mr. Pinkerton's class. *or*
So, today was *not* a good day at school.

More Complex Forms of Accepting

There are also more advanced forms of conveying acceptance, such as summarizing, labeling feelings, affirming and admiring, providing warmth and affection, and engaging in parent–child play. Some are slightly more complex ways to show you're paying attention, and others take a different approach to convey a message of belonging. These are described next.

SUMMARIZE

Periodically summarizing what you see your children doing is a great way to show that you're paying attention and trying to understand them. It's not a difficult skill to use; it's just difficult to remember to use it. Here are some examples:

- "I noticed you hardly ever talk to your friends on the phone; I guess you'd rather text back and forth."
- "I see that you often do math homework before you do spelling."
- "I noticed you sit in this chair when you watch TV."
- "When your friends are here, you play *Call of Duty*. But when you're by yourself, you play other games."

You can also summarize what your child *says*. Summarizing is particularly valuable when you're listening to children tell a story or explain a problem that is long, complicated, or emotional. Again, summarizing is not hard to do; it's just hard to remember to do. Here is an example of a parent who paraphrases and then summarizes at the end:

> *Child:* School sucks. And Mr. Pinkerton is a jerk. Why did I have to get him for a teacher?
>
> *You:* So, not a good day at school.
>
> *Child:* No. Not at all! What is the deal with Mr. Pinkerton? Why is he such a jerk?
>
> *You:* You *really* don't like him.
>
> *Child:* He's rude, he plays favorites, and he's got it in for me. Don't ask me why.
>
> *You:* That doesn't sound good.
>
> *Child:* No, it isn't. Do I have to go to school tomorrow? I hate school!
>
> *You:* Wow. Let me see if I got all this: You don't like Mr. Pinkerton, you don't like how he treats students, and now you hate school and don't want to go.

LABEL FEELINGS

A more advanced way to show that you're listening and trying to understand is to try to label your child's feelings. There are several advantages to doing this; for now, the point is that it can show just how close you're following along and how hard you're trying to understand your child. But be careful: Your labels should be very tentative, mere educated guesses that could be right or wrong. And whether you're right or wrong is not that important. The main thing is that you're listening, paying attention, and trying to get to know your children. Here are examples of parents labeling their child's feelings:

- "You think it's funny that I text so slow!"
- "You're mad because you couldn't figure out that last math problem."
- "You look sad. Are you missing your friends?"
- "You seemed nervous going into the dentist's office."

AFFIRM AND ADMIRE

When used consistently and earnestly, affirmation and admiration do a good job of letting children know they're valued in your eyes and fully belong in your family. Here are examples of parents using affirmation or admiration:

- "You are amazingly quick with your text messaging!"
- "I'm really proud of how hard you're working on your math."
- "It's fun to watch you laugh at the funny things on this TV show."
- "It's nice of you to play with your little brother."
- "You know, you're really polite when you speak to adults you don't know."

WARMTH AND AFFECTION

Hugs, a pat on the shoulder, a kiss on the head, or lying down and leafing through a magazine together are all useful ways to say, "You matter to me." Of course, not all parents are warm and fuzzy, and not all children want parents to be warm and fuzzy. There are also times when you don't feel like hugging or kissing your children. That's certainly the case when children are being defiant and disrespectful or hurting others and breaking things. Still, warmth and affection, like affirmation and admiration, are useful options for conveying a message of belonging.

PARENT–CHILD PLAY

For parents of young children, an ideal time to convey a message of acceptance is when they're playing. In fact, science-based interventions for young children with behavior problems (around age 2–7 years) routinely ask parents to set time aside each day or week for parent–child play. The aim is to build a stronger parent–child relationship, which means the goal is not for parents to play with their children but to be *with* their children as they play. During this kind of play, a parent's job is to follow their child's lead. Forget teaching, preaching, and correcting. Imagine doing this on a regular basis—create a special play time for your child and a chance for you to listen and follow along as your child plays (see the suggested guidelines for this kind of play). Parents with older children might need to find other ways to spend time together (e.g., running errands, making breakfast on Saturday morning, making homemade pizza each week), but the same principles apply: Listen, follow, and accept. Consider creating a miniritual (see Chapter 4) that you can put on your weekly or monthly schedule as a reminder to spend focused time with each of your children. There are few gifts more valuable to them. If done regularly, in small doses (because it's all they need and all you can do), your children will come to relish the time and attention you give them.

 Lauren's View

The power of parent–child play comes from parents giving the gifts of time and attention. For some children, the only way to get these precious gifts is by misbehaving. I often prompt parents of young children to notice what happens after their children misbehave. For example, what do they do after throwing a toy or knocking something off a table? Do they look to their parents for a reaction? Research has shown that parent attention is often the reward "earned" by misbehaving children.

Guidelines for Parent–Child Play

Before Play

- Schedule a regular time when you can be with your child as they play. Aim for around 30 minutes, but less is fine if it's done consistently.
- Turn off all distractions (e.g., TV, music, phones).
- Bring out toys and games chosen especially for this play time.
  - Find toys that are good for fun and creativity (e.g., play dough, blocks, dolls, puppets).
  - When engaging in more structured activities (e.g., board games), remember that following the child is more important than following the rules of the game.
  - Avoid toys and games that children find very engaging regardless of whether their parents are present (e.g., video games).
- Set a timer.
- If you're feeling tense, remember to take a few deep breaths (in through your nose for 4 seconds, then out through your mouth for 5 seconds or more).

During Play

- Here's a useful script when starting: "This is our special play time. While we're playing, you can choose what to play and what to say. If there's something you can't do, I'll let you know."
- Sit near or next to your child, even if it means sitting on the floor.
- Look, listen, and follow their lead as they begin to play.
- Use facial expressions to show you're listening and watching their play.
- Hold back the urge to correct, criticize, help, or change the play, even if the game rules are ignored.
- Use reflective listening skills.
  - Describe (play-by-play) what your child is doing: "You're using the blocks to make a tower."
  - Repeat back what your child has said.

> *Child:* This is so hard.
> *Parent:* This *is* hard.

(continues)

Guidelines for Parent–Child Play (*Continued*)

- Summarize what your child has said.

> *Child:* Playdough is fun, but it makes my hands dirty. I want to play with the blocks, but it's still on my hands. I *like* to stack my blocks *really* high and then crash them, but they keep falling down before I can stack them *super* high!
>
> *Parent:* Playdough and blocks are both fun but different.

- Comment on what your child might be feeling: "It sounds like you're pretty frustrated because the tower keeps falling before you can knock it down."
- If your child hurts you or damages something, calmly give a warning that play will end if it happens again. If it does happen again, end the play for that day.
- When the kitchen timer sounds, announce to your child, "We have 5 more minutes to play."

After Play

- When it is time to end, announce, "Play time is over."
- If your child doesn't want to stop playing, reflect their feelings ("You are sad that play time is over. I had a lot of fun with you too!").
- Start putting the toys away (do not insist on their help, but praise them if they do!).

A Posture of Acceptance

If acceptance is to become your default mode of parenting, then it can't be used sparingly, sporadically, or only when your child is having emotional or behavioral problems. Acceptance doesn't work that way. Acceptance is a fundamental way to *be as a parent* and a fundamental way to *be with your child*. If children are to receive a message of belonging, it must be an integral part of who you are and how you interact with them. It can't be a thing used every now and then that is fun and exciting but perhaps also confusing. A message of belonging must be delivered sincerely and consistently through the rough spots of parenting—child misbehavior, developmental turmoil, family conflict, and all the rest. In short, if acceptance is to be your default mode of your parenting, then you'll need to adopt a *posture of acceptance*.

For some parents, a posture of acceptance can mean a radically different way to think, feel, and do the job of parenting. It means no longer thinking that your job is to fix every wrong or prevent every bad thing that could happen to your child, whether it's helping your son pour a glass of milk, correcting your daughter's mispronunciations, reminding children to brush their teeth, or refereeing when two siblings are arguing. When you adopt a posture of acceptance, your abiding assumption is that intervening will be the exception and not the rule. Of course, age, temperament, and context will determine where you set your threshold for stepping in and taking over. But be careful about assuming that *your* child is an exception to the acceptance rule, that they need more help, more correcting, and more guidance than other children. That could be true, but there's also a risk of getting stuck in a rut of hovering and overparenting. Consider a study in which researchers observed parents and kindergarten children eating dinner together (Orrell-Valente et al., 2007). The results showed that 85% of parents tried to get their children to eat more food and 83% of children ate more food than they would have without parents' prompts. It seemed that parents were inadvertently training children to eat past their internal hunger cues. Based on these findings, the researchers suggested that children, not parents, should decide what and how much they eat. That is true for many things in children's lives.

A posture of acceptance means an end to parental hovering. Picture it this way: Imagine standing up, turning away from your child, and going about your day. You're prepared to intervene but only when and if it is needed. A posture of acceptance also means managing whatever feelings show up when you're fighting the urge to help or intervene. As we discussed in Chapter 3, so much of what we do as parents is in service of our own emotions. We help a child pour a glass of milk because we don't like feeling anxious about the possible mess she could make. We correct a mispronunciation because we worry it will lead to our son being teased by peers. We remind our children to brush their teeth because we feel better when we check off these items from our nightly to-do list. A posture of acceptance means finding a different way to be with your children and a more adaptive way to manage the emotions of parenting. Our hope is that some of those ways will include providing your children with explicit, consistent messages of belonging. The range of options is broad, so you should be able to find one that provides minimal coverage but maximum sustainability for your message of belonging.

Some parents can operate easily and naturally from a posture of acceptance, but others will see it as an uncomfortable departure from the status quo. It can also be a difficult concept to understand and implement, and some parents have a hard time allowing themselves to pull back far enough and long

 Tim's View

One of my graduate students did a study in which we looked at different ways to train parents to use play to be more accepting. Participants were mothers and their boys (ages 4–6). One group watched a video on how to play with a child in a way that was accepting. Another group did that *and* practiced doing it with feedback on their performance. A third group did all that *and* had a chance to "process" (discuss with the trainer) what they were thinking and feeling as they played in this way with their child. Only the last group showed any real differences from mothers who had no training. It seems that for some parents, a posture of acceptance can be a hard thing to get their head around.

enough to be accepting. Consider these comments from a study of parents who just completed their 20th parenting class. In the first comment, a father sees the importance of giving his child space—a lesson about acceptance that he learned not so much from the training but from the skilled trainer.

> You know, something we haven't talked about specifically in this parenting class, although it is in everything you've talked about, is respecting children and their space in the world. You know they should be treated as human beings—it doesn't mean you don't set limits and all that stuff. But it means you know that they're human beings and as deserving of respect as you are.

In the next comment, a mother also mentions giving her child space but adds a point about looking into her child's eyes:

> In the last 3 weeks, I've noticed a synthesis of all the sessions we've had and me basically changing the way I interact with Hannah [my daughter] in a dramatic way—spontaneously. Now when I interact with her, I tend to look at her eyes and I realize I can't remember my parents ever doing that. I'm giving her more space and time—more room to make mistakes, screw up, and make messes. I'm trying to give her more independence; when she wants to do something, let her do it rather than saying you're going to spill the milk all over the floor. It's fine if she spills the milk; she'll learn what happens. And we've actually been getting on really well.

These are impressive insights into the posture of acceptance. These parents realized that acceptance isn't simply creating positive, happy moments; it's about sustained changes in how they related to their child. As you become more comfortable and consistent in using various acceptance options, you could experience a similar shift in how you "see" your child and how you experience your relationship with your child.

POTENTIAL OBSTACLES

Sometimes obstacles get in the way of parents being more accepting. We generally encounter two types. One involves parents using poor substitutes for accepting, and the other involves parents questioning the value of being accepting. An example of the first type of obstacle is when parents confuse acceptance with really fun events, special outings (e.g., going to an amusement park), or expensive gifts. Some parents use big, showy actions to convince children they are valued or to soften their own guilt about not giving children more time and attention. Be careful about investing in big activities or expensive things. It is far better to invest fully in your child and in your relationship with your child.

Another commonly used substitute for acceptance is rewarding children for certain behaviors. This is a frequently recommended parenting strategy: Children get a reward when they do a particular thing, do it a certain way (go to bed on time without backtalk), or do it a certain number of times (go to bed on time 4 days this week). A lot of things can be rewards: praise (You did an amazing job listening!), privileges (15 extra minutes of outdoor play before bed), or prizes (ice cream cone, book). Using rewards in this way is highly effective for helping children learn and practice behaviors that are new, difficult, or both. Examples might be finishing their homework, staying in bed at night, and doing household chores. But there are important differences between rewarding children for how they behave and conveying to children a sincere message of acceptance and belonging. Acceptance does not depend on children's use of certain behaviors. It's the default mode of parenting. It's there 24/7. It doesn't have to be earned. This point will make more sense when we discuss containing in Chapter 6.

The other common obstacle to adopting a posture of acceptance is to doubt its value. We've worked with a number of parents for whom discussions about acceptance must have seemed like we were speaking in a new tongue. This is more likely to happen with parents whose own childhood lacked acceptance or was marked by abuse, neglect, or psychological control. It can be hard—but not impossible—to make sense of and convey acceptance if you haven't experienced it as a child. If you're one of these parents, we encourage you to start slow, perhaps beginning with the simpler options for conveying acceptance, such as being still and quiet with your child. Practicing acceptance is way more helpful than trying to reason your way to acceptance. We also wouldn't recommend waiting to

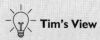

Tim's View

I've worked with parents whose difficult childhood led to struggles with both emotions and relationships. When their goal is to parent differently than how they were parented, I find that practicing parent–child play is more effective than talking about their childhood. Directly experiencing the thoughts and emotions that arise when parents are learning how to be accepting of their children can be very powerful.

feel more accepting toward your children. Instead, take small steps and *behave* your way to an enduring posture of acceptance. It can also help to practice strategies for managing the emotions that come with parenting (Chapter 3).

Some parents question the value of acceptance. They see it as silly or counterproductive, and they're not always wrong. For example, if children are frequently violent and hurting other family members, acceptance should wait until other steps are in place to stop or reduce violent actions. We should also note that for children with a developmental delay or a pervasive developmental disorder (e.g., autism), a message of acceptance could look different from that used with other children. For example, your child may not want you to tell them at length about how you accept them. Instead, engaging in their special interest may be a more effective tool. There are also some parents who view acceptance as being lazy or neglectful or as giving in and being weak. This is especially likely if parents rely heavily on micromanaging their children's lives to prevent any emotional or behavioral problems. This approach to parenting seems to be saying, "If everyone just cooperated, we wouldn't have any problems and I could relax!" There are also parents who believe that the main job of parenting is to teach important life lessons, make children tough or tough-minded, or protect them from harm and pain. If any of these descriptions apply to you, consider that it's also important to equip children with a capacity to solve their own problems. Thus, children need opportunities to work through challenging problems, which is more likely when you adopt a posture of acceptance. Our suggestion is to look for opportunities when children can practice solving problems on their own.

Try this the next time your daughter or son comes to you with a problem or concern. Listen carefully without interrupting, say out loud what they seem to be feeling (e.g., "You seem sad or maybe disappointed"), and then ask this question, with all seriousness: "What are you going to do?" In our experience, this rarely asked question is one of the more helpful "lines" a parent could ever use. Packed within it are several powerful messages for your child. It says, "I understand that what you're dealing with is hard, and I believe you can solve it on your own. I'll be here if you need me, but I'm also curious what you're going to do." It's also a message for the parent, which says this:

> My child is upset or confused, and it worries me. I'll fight the urge to fix my child's problem so I can give an even greater gift—the gift of witnessing their persistence and celebrating their success when the issue is managed on their own. It might look like I'm not helping, but the truth is I'll be helping in a different, better way.

POTENTIAL WINS

The gains that come from a posture of acceptance are significant and numerous. Unfortunately, most are neither obvious nor immediate. One that might occur right away is that your child is more cooperative and obedient. Several studies show that children, on average, are more obedient after their parents are trained to be more accepting. Scientists aren't sure why this happens, and there's no guarantee that it will happen with your child, but it might! Other gains that follow from a posture of acceptance are more delayed but can include these positive changes:

- increased self-worth,
- ability to regulate their emotions,
- likelihood of adopting their parents' values, and
- likelihood of understanding a message of containment.

You may have heard this expression: "To know me is to love me." That's not always the case for strong-willed children whose defiant or disruptive behavior can make it hard to like them ("I love my child, but I don't like my child"). If parents don't take the time to get to know their children, children could begin to question their self-worth. They could become resigned to the "fact" that their parents are too busy, have their own concerns, or just don't "get" them.

When parents operate from a posture of acceptance, children learn to better regulate their emotions. Parents' use of reflective listening is particularly helpful when coaching children through emotionally tough times. Imagine, for example, your teenage daughter calling at 9:00 p.m. on a Friday to ask if she could stay the night at a friend's house. You remind her that your family has to leave town early the next morning to visit grandparents, so she'll have to come home. She's not happy with your answer and rails angrily about how everybody else's parents were okay with staying over. As a parent, you could certainly find reason to focus on her ugly tirade and her insensitivity to the needs of the family. But it's also an opportunity to help her better

139

Tim's View

I see a lot of these kinds of children in my practice. Some might exaggerate the extent to which parents are clueless or uncaring, but the effect is often the same. Parents who are accepting convey a message of being open and eager to learn about their child's life. They create opportunities (e.g., one-on-one time) and reduce obstacles (e.g., criticism, lectures, excessive work) that prevent them from getting to know their children. When parents become more accepting, children often experience a boost in self-esteem, which is not surprising: Nothing is as powerful as a consistent and earnest effort to get to know your child (certainly not material goods, or even praise, hugs, or kisses). Take the time to learn about the world your children live in, how they are doing, and what their struggles might be. When you know all that *and* you're still there and still accepting, there is no bigger gift.

manage emotions such as disappointment, frustration, and anger. Here is an example of how a *nonaccepting parent* might handle a tough situation:

Child: What do you mean I can't stay over?

You: I said you can't, and that's final. Now get your things together!

Child: Mom! That is so unfair!

You: Oh, you think it is unfair, huh? I give you everything and this is the thanks I get? You are acting like a nasty, spoiled brat right now.

Child: It *is* unfair! Everybody else is spending the night. I'm the only one that's not!

You: I don't care! You complain like this is the worst thing in the world. There are so many people who have it so much harder than you do. Stop feeling sorry for yourself!

Child: You are the WORST! I'm not leaving!

You: Don't take that tone with me, young lady! I'll grab you right now and you can go without your phone for the rest of the month! You are disrespecting me and your grandparents.

Child: UGH! I hate you! And I hate this family!

You: I'm getting you right now and then we can see what you have to say for yourself.

As we discussed in Chapter 3, anger is a quick emotion that often rises to the surface during challenging situations. When we are prodded, anger can flare easily and can lead to arguments that aren't helpful for the parent–child relationship. But if you are able to put your own anger aside and also validate how your child is feeling, it is easier to see the other emotions that might be at play for your child and you. By accepting your child's emotions, it makes it easier to connect to one another. Now, here is an example of how an accepting parent might handle this situation:

Child: What do you mean I can't stay over?

You: It just won't work out tonight. We're leaving too early in the morning. I need you home this evening.

Child: Mom! That is so unfair!

You: I know it seems unfair, but we planned this trip a month ago.

Child: But everybody else is spending the night. I'm the only one that's not.

You: I know you're disappointed.

Child: Can't you come get me early tomorrow morning?

You: I'm sorry, honey. We have too much to do in the morning to get ready. I can't come get you tomorrow.

> *Child:* This really sucks! Now I've got to tell everybody
> that I'm the only one having to go home. That's
> so embarrassing.
> *You:* You hate being the only one who has to leave.
> *Child:* Well, yeah. Just so we can visit my stupid grand-
> parents.
> *You:* It doesn't seem fair, does it?
> *Child:* No, it's not! [*She starts crying.*]
> *You:* I'm sorry, honey. I know this is hard for you.
> *Child:* So you'll come get me now?
> *You:* Sure. I'm on my way.

Despite the unpleasantness of this exchange, it represents an important teachable moment. Consider all that transpired in this example.
This mom allowed her daughter to express her emotions so she can
learn to live with and accept emotions rather than deny or avoid
them. She labeled her daughter's emotions to help her recognize what
she was feeling. She let her daughter know that it's normal and understandable to have those feelings. Finally, she helped her daughter slow
down and learn that her feelings carry potentially useful information
that can be used to make a wise plan. It takes longer to reflect and
label your children's feelings than it does to tell them to be quiet and
quit their whining. But when you coach them through these emotional moments, they learn valuable skills that can last a lifetime.

We should also point out that there's no need for parents to give
in to bad behavior just because they're acknowledging and reflecting
their child's feelings. Notice that the mother in the example wasn't
swayed by her daughter's demands. (In the next chapter, we'll have
more to say about how parents can combine reflective listening and
behavioral limit setting.) There might even be times when parents'
efforts to reflect children's feelings are rewarded by children pulling
back from misbehavior such as defiance. This won't happen every

time, and it's not the primary reason for reflecting and labeling children's feelings, but it's nice when it happens. Think of it this way: When our children are very young and they fall apart emotionally, we soothe them by holding, nursing, or rocking them. When our children are older, strategies for soothing are more verbal than physical. So, if you want to soothe your children with your words to *possibly* settle them down, try words that let them know you understand how they feel, ideally in a calm, supportive, and reassuring voice.

Parents who are accepting tend to matter more to their children than parents who aren't accepting. That means you are more likely to get your children to buy in to beliefs you hold dear and to expectations you have for them. Several studies support this. One found that when mothers were accepting, children were more likely to obey the mothers' rules even when mothers weren't there to enforce these rules. So, if character is what you do when no one is looking, then accepting parents are apt to have children with higher moral character.

The last benefit to mention is that a posture of acceptance is an ideal contrast to when parents shift into "containment mode." In the next chapter, we discuss the topic of containing, but we encourage you to recognize the important link between accepting and containing. To discipline is to teach; one lesson we teach our children is the difference between right and wrong, what's allowed and not allowed. When parents combine a posture of acceptance with firm but selective discipline, their children have a much easier time distinguishing between what's allowed and not allowed.

ACCEPTANCE HOMEWORK

- Revisit the Listen and Follow section in this chapter.
- Try this experiment: Use simple accepting skills (parroting, paraphrasing, and describing what you see) a couple of days for a week to try it out and to see how your children respond.

- Listen for opportunities to label and reflect your child's feelings.
- Make notes of when and how you show (a) affirmation and admiration and (b) warmth and affection to your children.
- If you have younger children, consider engaging in a bit of "floor time" for parent–child play.
- Ask your children what it's like having you as a parent. Use their response to gauge whether you're parenting from a posture of acceptance.

CHAPTER 6

CONTAIN: EFFECTIVE DISCIPLINE IS SELECTIVE DISCIPLINE

It's often said that children need structure and limits so they can learn the difference between right and wrong. William Golding made that point in *Lord of the Flies*. In the story, the boys' tragic turn toward savagery comes to an end when a military ship arrives and the boys are chided by a naval officer—one trained to inflict his own brand of savagery. The question of whether humans are innately aggressive has long been debated by philosophers, theologians, and scientists. Psychologists generally answer the question by saying that some individuals are more prone to aggression than others, but most children will grow to become healthy, nonviolent, productive members of their community. If you're a parent whose child is very strong-willed or even defiant and disrespectful, a chapter on setting limits might be the first (or only) chapter you read. We hope not, but if it is, be aware that your capacity to *contain* your child's misbehavior is only one third of what's needed for a strong, healthy parent–child relationship; parents also need to accept and lead.

This chapter aims to help you

- understand what it means to contain children's behavior,
- learn how to use containing with accepting,
- learn to use the Disciplinary Funnel,

- learn the key components of an adaptive containment script, and
- build your own four-step approach to containment.

WHAT IS CONTAINING?

Why *contain*? We could have used the term *discipline*, but that term means vastly different things to different parents. We also want you to be newly curious about this topic because we approach it in ways that are distinct from what you might have read or heard elsewhere. The term *containing* conveys a message of restraint. If spoken aloud by parents, the message might sound like this: "You're my child and a part of this family. And there are some things I cannot let you do." You'll notice parallels between this definition and that for *accepting*. That's because both involve providing children with a clear, important message.

In our research, we tried to measure the degree to which young people have a sense of containment—a belief that a person in authority (e.g., parent, teacher) has the capacity to hold them accountable and limit their behavior. In fact, we've developed measures for both children and for college students. In doing so, we assumed that few children or college students would believe they had greater power than the adults in charge. Here are sample questions from scales used to assess containment beliefs. The first question is from the child scale and the second question is from the college student scale.

- You want to play with some friends outside. Your mom says you can't go. Can she make you stay inside?
- You are standing in the express line at Walmart. You have 20 items and the maximum allowed is 15. The store clerk tells you that you must change lanes due to being over the limit. Can she make you move to a different checkout lane?

The good news is that most of the children studied, even among those identified by teachers and peers as aggressive, believed that parents and teachers were in charge. Moreover, for them, better parental discipline predicted less antisocial behavior. However, for children and college students who lacked a sense of containment, there was a greater likelihood of engaging in antisocial acts. Importantly, for children with a low sense of containment, parent discipline mattered little when predicting their aggressive and antisocial behavior: These children had high levels of disruptive behavior regardless of how well their parents disciplined. In short, these children—not their parents—were calling the shots, only their choices weren't good ones.

CONTAINING *WITH* ACCEPTING

Much of what children learn about right and wrong comes from what parents do or do not allow. It's a system that works well in most families: Parents have certain expectations, children meet those expectations, everyone's okay with the arrangement, and children grow up to be good citizens. But some children have a harder time learning from their parents' discipline. It's also true that some parents have a harder time being consistent in what they expect from children. Not surprisingly, these types of children and parents are often in the same family, which is another example of how children can influence parents, and not just the reverse.

Research has shown that parents whose children are frequently defiant and disruptive tend to shift back and forth between being overly punitive and overly permissive. Parents do this because nothing seems to work for very long. The usual system of having expectations for children's behavior and children meeting those expectations doesn't seem to apply; instead, parents are not clear or consistent in their expectations and children aren't reliably held to parents' expectations. Parents who struggle with this dilemma are often advised by professionals to use *effective* discipline, but what does that mean? The theme of this chapter is that **effective discipline is selective discipline.** Parents hear often about the former but less about the latter. So, in this chapter, we provide a path to using selective discipline. The gist is this: When parents believe that the chief task of parenting is to make children obedient, they overvalue discipline and undervalue acceptance. An overly broad and harsh approach to discipline undermines the goal of combining containment and acceptance, which is core to our holistic, long-term model of parenting.

Selective Discipline

It could be said that discipline is *selective* when parents "choose their battles wisely." This is a commonly used phrase, but it's also rather vague and potentially misleading. We don't see discipline as a battle that parents must wage with children, which is one more reason we prefer the term *contain.* Also unclear is how parents are supposed to choose their disciplinary "battles." Consider the commonly held belief that children should obey their parents. For many parents, this is a basic assumption (Truth with a capital T), but it can also be a stumbling block for children who didn't get the "obey-your-parents" memo. Not all children are predisposed to be obedient and cooperative. Some come with a tendency to challenge parents and have strong emotions; obedience is not their strong suit. Even generally obedient children can have bad days or rough patches when they're not so cooperative. So, the question remains: Which battles do you fight and which do you let go?

We assume most parents adjust their expectations to fit children's age and temperament. But we also suspect this is done in a trial-and-error sort of way. For example, let's say that on Day 1, you ask your son to make his bed but he doesn't do it. You ask him on Day 2 to make his bed and he still doesn't do it, only this time you remind him three times and he eventually does it. On Day 3, you forget to tell him to make his bed and he doesn't do it, although he "knows" he's supposed to do it and you know he knows. On Day 4, you hesitate before telling him to make his bed because you're trying to figure out what you'll do if he doesn't obey: Will you follow through and make him do it or will you let it slide because it's not worth the hassle? When you live with children who are defiant and disruptive, this scenario can happen multiple times a day! It's easy for their parents to feel burned out, having suffered too many defeats from trying to enforce this or that expectation. Selective discipline involves parents **recognizing that there are limits to what they can expect from children *and* letting some things go while staying focused on what matters most.** If parents are to navigate the long-term job of parenting, they must be selective about when and where they use their energy. Yes, it would be nice if you wake up in the morning and your children didn't get their new shirt dirty right before school, they brushed their teeth after breakfast, they didn't dawdle when getting dressed, or they didn't roll

Tim's View

I used to referee high school basketball. Oddly, it's a lot like being a parent who uses selective discipline. Less experienced referees tend to over-officiate, anticipating fouls and violations that never happen. Experienced referees settle back and assume each game will be played without the need to blow their whistle. That doesn't happen, of course, but when a foul or a violation occurs, it comes almost as a surprise, something that stands out and is important to point out. So, experienced referees don't miss the obvious fouls or violations. The same holds true for parenting. Trust that when the time comes and the need arises, you'll be ready to contain your child's misbehavior. Don't be fooled by the belief that your child's future is in jeopardy unless you're hypervigilant and ready to teach and correct at the slightest misdeed.

their eyes and complain when told it was time to leave. Each of these could be a disciplinary "battle," but too much discipline can interfere with your efforts to be accepting. Being overly punitive can slowly erode the quality of the parent–child relationship, which is the best tool in parenting. Being systematic about how and when to handle misbehavior is also essential if parents are to have the energy needed to be effective disciplinarians when it matters.

Effective Discipline

A useful way to think about *effective discipline* is to view it as parenting actions that raise the cost of children's misbehavior. This is a rather technical point but it's hugely important: If containment is to be effective, it should "cost" your child more when they do *not* meet your expectations than when they do meet your expectations. Conversely, the reward or benefit of meeting your expectations should outweigh the benefits of *not* meeting your expectations. Children, like nearly all humans, tend to behave in ways that match the rate of being rewarded or punished. If we could get paid for surfing the internet or for putting in 8 hours of physical labor, guess which choice most of us would make? Similarly, if your children can do the dishes quickly so they can watch their favorite TV show *or* complain loudly for 30 seconds and avoid the dishes altogether, they're likely to go with complaining. Note that we're not implying this would be a conscious choice on their part (though it might be); instead, we're saying that human behavior is greatly shaped by what is rewarded and what is punished—what "works" and what "doesn't work." We all share the tendency for our behavior to match the contingencies that are available. To behave in ways that run counter to the reinforcing or punishing consequences of our actions is more difficult and less common, which is why it's hard to quit smoking or stop eating snacks, especially if cigarettes and snacks are readily available.

Our way of defining effective discipline helps explain the importance of blending containment with acceptance. In the context of an accepting parent–child relationship, children will have less reason and less motivation to break rules or misbehave because they feel accepted and are more connected to family. Thus, they are more likely to buy into household rules and family values. Again, it's the same for adults; we complain less and work harder when we feel valued at work and are compensated fairly. But if we're treated badly or paid little, then we're not so enthusiastic about work. In families where there is little acceptance, where children are routinely criticized and frequently punished, getting them to do a simple task can be hard—unless it's done out of fear. Thus, for some children, defiance and coercion are the most reliable strategies for getting something they want.

THE FIXED-RATIO SYSTEM

A more systematic way to adjust your expectations as a parent—to choose your "battles" wisely—is to adopt a *fixed-ratio approach* to discipline. This is an approach that recognizes that parents' efforts to follow through with discipline can, at times, lead to conflict, harsh words, or hurt

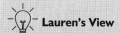 **Lauren's View**

You may be wondering, "How in the world do I make 80% of my interactions with my child positive or neutral?" As a parent of toddlers, I appreciate this question! I spend a lot of time keeping my children from unintentionally hurting themselves or breaking something (i.e., natural toddler behaviors). That means many of our interactions could make them sad or mad ("Why can't I jump from the top of the couch to the coffee table?"). But it's important to remember that 80% can be positive *or* neutral, and letting things go is one type of neutral interaction (e.g., not commenting when your child says, "I don't like your dumb rule"). A well-chosen *nonresponse* can be incredibly useful to parents.

feelings. Disciplinary interactions are often necessary, but too many disciplinary encounters can undermine the goal of acceptance. The fixed-ratio system is based on research showing that the ratio of emotionally positive (or neutral) interactions to emotionally negative interactions is an important consideration in any relationship: Relationships are generally more stable and more satisfying when there are more positive interactions than negative interactions. Researchers find that a ratio between 4:1 and 8:1 is optimal. We generally ask parents to aim for a 4:1 ratio because it's easier to obtain, especially for families with children who might be difficult or disruptive. So, for every negative interaction you have with your children, it's helpful to have at least four positive or neutral interactions. This means that roughly 80% of your interactions with your child will be positive or neutral and only about 20% will be negative.

In some families, the parent–child relationship is not at a 4:1 ratio; instead, it's more like 1:1 (or lower), which means half of all parent–child interactions are negative. If that describes your relationship with your child, staying at a 1:1 ratio could jeopardize the quality of the relationship and your child's growth and development. Children need a disciplinary approach that is forceful enough to restrict their involvement in serious misbehavior but not so forceful that it undermines a consistent message of

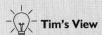

Tim's View

Perhaps you've been in a romantic relationship in which the ratio of positive to negative interactions was 1:1. When this happens, the bond between you and your partner is only as good as your last interaction or your next interaction. You're constantly one hurtful comment or one mismanaged argument away from being in the red (more negative than positive). There is no positive relationship credit to buffer against missteps, so every interaction is a test and every negative encounter is like a wound to the relationship.

acceptance. Consider how the fixed-ratio system can be applied to your parenting. What will have to change if your discipline efforts are to become both selective *and* effective?

With a fixed-ratio system, your efforts to limit child misbehavior are fixed or constrained by the level of positivity in the parent–child relationship, which, of course, can vary widely from one family to the next. When the parent–child relationship is strained and children don't feel accepted, parents must be highly selective in their approach to discipline. They might have lots of excellent reasons for why their children should, say, turn off the lights when they leave a room, not bring food into the living room, spend less time watching TV, or a dozen other things, but those reasons won't matter if the emotional tone of the relationship is negative and weighed down from repeated attempts to enforce all those expectations. Now, if your family happens to be one where children are sweet and cooperative and you are generally laid back and agreeable, then you can probably expect all these things and still maintain a 4:1 ratio. In fact, in these kinds of families, the fixed-ratio system is barely noticeable: Parents hold high expectations, children meet those expectations, and the relationship is no worse for the wear. But not all parents are this lucky. So, don't be surprised if you need to let go of certain expectations (e.g., making the bed every morning, doing homework without being asked) if you're going to reach and maintain a 4:1 ratio. In other words, you might have to settle for a rather short list of child behaviors that warrant discipline.

You also might be thinking, "How positive do the positive parent–child interactions need to be?" To be honest, not much. There's no need to be sweet and affectionate 24/7, which, frankly, is unrealistic, especially for working parents with multiple children. In fact, a better question is, "How can I avoid emotionally *negative or unpleasant* interactions?" The quick answer is you can't, not entirely. But it is important to be mindful of the impact harsh parenting can have on children's development. We humans are wired to be more attuned to events that produce unpleasant feelings (e.g., fear, sadness) than to events that produce pleasant feelings. That has helped us stay alive in the face of danger and threat. But that capacity also means negative parent–child interactions carry lots of emotional weight. Imagine enjoying a fun trip to the grocery store with your kids and then getting very angry when they do something that upsets you. That one brief, harsh interaction has the potential to outweigh the other 60 minutes of fun you had with your children. Ugly, unfortunate parenting encounters cannot be prevented entirely; all parents have the potential to misstep and react harshly at times. Later we address the importance of *reconnecting* with your child and *repairing* the relationship after a difficult disciplinary encounter. For now, the key takeaway is that *effective* discipline is *selective* discipline.

THE DISCIPLINARY FUNNEL

Parents will differ on how they achieve and maintain a 4:1 ratio of positive/neutral to negative parent–child interactions. The key is discerning what you can reasonably expect of your children and how selective you need to be with your discipline. Some parents can expect way more than others. Figure 6.1 presents the *Disciplinary Funnel*, which can be used to determine how selective you should be if you're going to maintain a healthy ratio of positive to negative exchanges. This funnel presents potential disciplinary targets along with a guide for setting your expectations. A *disciplinary target* is a behavior that (a) you expect of your child and (b) are willing to insist on 100% of the time (or as close to 100% as you can get). We use a funnel in Figure 6.1 to show that your disciplinary focus will get increasingly narrow as you move further down the list of expectations.

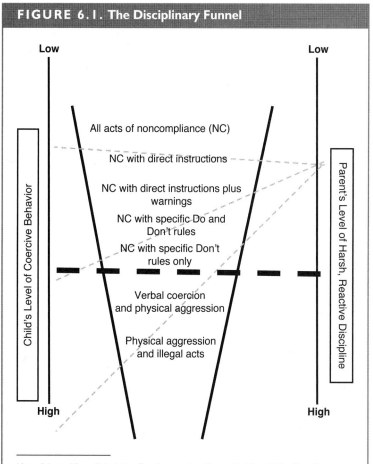

FIGURE 6.1. The Disciplinary Funnel

Low   Low

Child's Level of Coercive Behavior

Parent's Level of Harsh, Reactive Discipline

All acts of noncompliance (NC)

NC with direct instructions

NC with direct instructions plus warnings

NC with specific Do and Don't rules

NC with specific Don't rules only

Verbal coercion and physical aggression

Physical aggression and illegal acts

High   High

Note. Adapted from "Updating Our Approach to Parent Training. I: The Case Against Targeting Noncompliance," by T. A. Cavell, 2001, *Clinical Psychology: Science and Practice*, *8*(3), p. 313 (https://doi.org/10.1093/clipsy.8.3.299). Copyright 2001 by the American Psychological Association.

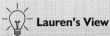

Lauren's View

Parents of young children often ask, "What do I do if I'm not addressing all of my child's misbehaviors?" The answer may shock some people, but ignoring is a pretty good, science-supported option. If your child is not in immediate danger, is not hurting themselves or someone else, and is not destroying property, it can help to simply ignore the misbehavior. Whining, yelling, tantrums, attitude, sarcasm, and other aggravating behaviors can all be ignored with little risk to your child's growth and development. In fact, the less attention you give to these lower level aggravating behaviors, the less you'll see of them. It's not always easy to ignore these kinds of misbehaviors, but it's a good strategy for getting to a 4:1 ratio.

Before we describe the Disciplinary Funnel and how to use it, consider first the implications of having a short list of disciplinary targets. What would be different if you had *just a few*, *very specific* expectations for your children's behavior, *but* you followed through or enforced these behaviors 100% of the time? For parents who seldom follow through with their discipline, it could mean working harder; but for other parents, it could mean working less hard. By allowing (or not chasing after) behaviors that are not on their short list, they greatly narrow their disciplinary focus. The result is less time and effort spent arguing with children every time they do something annoying or don't do what they're told to do. That's where a posture of acceptance can be a useful complement to containment: Instead of being primed to punish or correct most any misbehavior, parents who use selective discipline move toward containment only when it matters most. And once the disciplinary encounter is over, they're quick to resume a posture of acceptance and nonintervention.

The Disciplinary Funnel can help you identify disciplinary targets that are suited to the kind of relationship you have with your children. You'll need to consider two key factors: The first key factor is your child's level of misbehavior: How difficult, coercive, or antisocial are your child's actions day in and day out? This tells you how hard you'll have to work and how important it is to narrow your focus. Mild defiance every so often is neither serious nor demanding from a parent's point of view. But if children and teens are prone to violent outbursts, use illegal substances, or engage in other delinquent behavior, the stakes are high and so too is the level of difficulty for containing.

The second key factor is your own tendency to react to child misbehavior with harsh, overly punitive parenting. Maintaining a healthy ratio of positive to negative exchanges (containing plus accepting) means being honest with yourself about whether your children's misbehavior results in you "losing it" or "going off." Once you have a realistic appraisal of where you and your child stand on these two factors, you can use the funnel to identify the disciplinary targets that are right for you and your family. In Figure 6.1, you see three thin dashed lines. These lines illustrate the level of target behavior indicated for children at varying levels of coercive behavior (assuming a set level of harsh, reactive parenting); as the child's level of coercion increases, the disciplinary focus increasingly narrows and addresses a much smaller list of problem behaviors.

Using the Disciplinary Funnel

We understand that applying this funnel may seem complicated. Here, we provide some definitions so you can best determine what level of intervention makes the most sense for your family.

ALL ACTS OF NONCOMPLIANCE

At the top of the funnel is the option to target all acts of disobedience or noncompliance. This is a truly ambitious goal because it means parents are following through with a disciplinary sanction each time their child disobeys any rule or expectation.

Noncompliance With Direct Instructions

You can narrow the scope of your discipline if you limit disobedience to times when your children don't obey a direct instruction. There are many ways to communicate an expectation to your children. Some are not very forceful and don't really qualify as instructions. These include asking, wishing, wondering, and pleading ("Would you mind maybe grabbing your shoes off the floor and putting them by the front door when you have time?"). Frankly, it's not fair to expect children to obey weakly worded requests, and if you're asking a question, the answer could rightfully be "No." But if you issue a clear simple instruction ("Put your shoes by the front door now, please.") and they still don't obey, that's your cue to move forward with a disciplinary sanction.

Noncompliance With Direct Instructions Plus Warnings

At this level, children are given a second chance before parents follow through with discipline. The advantage to using this level is that you give children additional information about what to expect ("If you don't put your shoes by the front door, then you won't be able to play your game before dinner"). You're still committed to following through 100% of the time, but you'll reduce the number of occasions when that's needed because children now know what to expect.

Noncompliance With Specific Do and Don't Rules

At this level, you will be making an important shift in the way you discipline. Instead of expecting compliance with each of your commands or instructions, you'll expect compliance with a specific set of standing rules. There are two key advantages to this approach. The first is that you're putting definite boundaries around your expectations and choosing to let some things go. It's an explicit attempt to use selective discipline. If you set your rules wisely, you should have less disciplinary conflict. The second key advantage is that you save yourself lots of time, energy, and costs (physical, emotional) because you're restricting what you go after. But be aware that a common mistake parents make is setting rules that are overly broad or vague (e.g., "Show respect"). When your rules are unclear, it is hard for children to know what qualifies as breaking the rule, and it makes it hard for parents to enforce the rules 100% of the time. Remember, a disciplinary target is not just what you expect; it's also what you're willing to work for. We provide some commonly used and explicitly stated *Do and Don't rules* next. This list will give you an idea of how big or small you can make your own rules.

Sample Do and Don't Rules

Do Rules

- Put your dirty clothes in the hamper.
- Shut the front door when you come into or leave the house.
- Put your dirty dishes in the dishwasher.
- Get permission before saying "yes" to friends' invitations.
- Be home before 11:00 p.m. on weekends.

Don't Rules

- Don't hit your siblings.
- Don't bring food into your bedroom.
- Don't watch TV shows rated for mature audiences.
- Don't invite friends inside if no parents are home.
- Don't sneak out of the house at night.

Noncompliance With Specific Don't Rules Only

Some research suggests that Do rules are harder for parents to enforce and harder for children to learn and follow than Don't rules. Thus, if you narrow your disciplinary focus to Don't rules only, you and your children should experience an even further reduction in negative exchanges. The downside to using only Don't rules is that you might leave undefined what you expect of your children. Of course, in many situations, it is rather obvious what parents expect of children. Examples include where they can eat food if the bedroom is off limits or what they can watch on TV if shows for mature audiences are prohibited.

Verbal Coercion and Physical Aggression

Verbal coercion refers to threatening comments, hurtful criticisms, angry profanity, and the like. When directed at parents, verbal coercion is often viewed as disrespect (e.g., "I hate when you interrupt my TV shows," "You're so stupid!") or defiance (e.g., "No! I told you I'll come when my show is over!"). Physically aggressive acts include hitting, grabbing, biting, pinching, and kicking others. Destruction of property can also be included under physical aggression. In some homes, verbal coercion and physical aggression occur so seldom that parents shouldn't concern themselves with this type of disciplinary target. But if children are using verbal coercion and physical aggression as their primary strategy to get what they want,

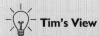
Tim's View

Aggression that starts in childhood is quite stable over time and carries significant risks. One group of researchers found that 50% of boys identified as aggressive by age 9 or 10 were arrested by the age of 14 (Patterson & Yoerger, 2002). Moreover, 75% of boys arrested by age 14 had three or more arrests by age 18.

then parents should take it seriously. Frequent use of coercive behavior can signal serious risk for such things as dropping out of school, delinquency, substance abuse, and risky sexual behavior.

As parents, you should focus your time and energy on addressing these behaviors before all others, if they're occurring. That's no small task, and it's made harder when parents feel powerless in the face of childhood coercion and aggression. We also caution parents about the challenge of setting limits on what their children say, even if it is mean

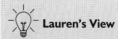

Lauren's View

If this describes one or more of your children, consider seeking professional help. Look for mental health care providers who use science-based approaches such as Parent–Child Interaction Therapy, Triple P–Positive Parenting, Incredible Years, Functional Family Therapy, Multisystemic Therapy, Generation-PMTO, or Brief Strategic Family Therapy.

and ugly. We issue this caution because it can be very difficult to control what comes out of a child's mouth, and you're not really using effective discipline if you can't contain what your child says. Yes, words can hurt but not nearly as much as physical aggression. Also, parents who try to stop children from making hurtful, vulgar, or disrespectful comments can soon find themselves trying to stop a long list

of unwanted verbalizations. It does help to specify exact words or phrases that are prohibited. Parents can even offer acceptable, perhaps humorous substitutes for "outlawed" words and comments: "I don't like when you say that, but you can say, *Oh, snap.*" But be careful. If you decide to take on your child's inappropriate or coercive language, you could be signing on to

Lauren's View

Studies of families with well-behaved children reveal that parents tend to ignore or deflect with humor much of the verbal coercion their children dish out (León-del-Barco et al., 2022).

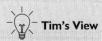

Tim's View

I've described this to parents as a kind of "verbal fishing" on the part of their children, hoping to "hook" their parents by their provocative words. I caution parents not to take the bait of kids throwing out an ugly comment, a biting criticism, or maybe a really bad curse word, followed by waiting to see how parents react. It's a tool that children can use to wield power and control.

Tim's View

A few parents with whom I've worked have settled into a pattern of living with a son or daughter who regularly flouts household rules, city ordinances, or state and local laws. They come to therapy because they are now the target of their child's aggressive or illegal acts. Doors are being broken, money is being stolen, and family members, including parents, are being hurt.

a long-term, losing battle. This is especially true when the words and phrases are designed to unnerve parents.

PHYSICAL AGGRESSION AND ILLEGAL ACTS

Physical aggression and illegal acts are at the very bottom of the Disciplinary Funnel. If your children are routinely engaging in these types of problem behaviors, you can't afford to be concerned about other matters. Focus your time and energy on these dangerous actions.

You can use the funnel to identify the behaviors that should be on your disciplinary short list—that list of target behaviors that ensure your use of selective discipline and help you maintain a 4:1 ratio in the parent–child relationship. Recognize also that the level of target behaviors identified by using the Disciplinary Funnel is merely an estimate: If you select a level but your disciplinary encounters are still occurring frequently, you can always drop down to a lower level. Some parents can stay at the top of the funnel, whereas others will need to start near the bottom of the funnel and perhaps work their way up over time.

If your child is displaying behaviors below the horizontal dashed line in Figure 6.1, the risks are significant and should warrant (a) immediate parental response (don't delay in recognizing these behaviors as unacceptable and deserving of a firm limit), (b) your highest attention (with limited/no wiggle room when imposing sanctions), and (c) possible expert intervention (e.g., family therapy with a mental health professional to help evaluate your family's involvement in a pattern of concern). If your child is displaying behaviors above the horizontal dashed line, it also makes sense to start with the most concerning behaviors (lower down in the funnel). The goal is not to address every misdeed but to conserve your disciplinary energy for the most developmentally significant misbehaviors.

Sadly, some parents come to tolerate their son or daughter being aggressive or engaging in delinquent acts. When these parents seek professional help, it's often because *they* are now the target of their child's antisocial behavior. Doors are being broken, money is being stolen, and parents are being pushed and slapped. Their children are also at risk for being arrested or placed out of the home, which can be scary and unpleasant. Indeed, some parents would rather tolerate a dissatisfying, debilitating relationship with a child who victimizes them than have that child placed out of the home for their safety.

There is no need to be your child's victim. No one benefits when parents are being hit, robbed, or vandalized. Children who routinely break laws and ignore rules against violence and victimization have lost sight of what their family values and what it believes. The Navajo have a saying for those who behave this way: "They act as if they had no relatives." At a minimum, family members should be kept safe, and parents have a responsibility to protect the health and well-being of their family members. If this is your family and you're a parent operating at the very bottom of the Disciplinary Funnel, it's probably time to get professional help. That help will likely involve a combination

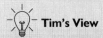

Tim's View

My own message to parents is some version of the following: "Refuse to be a victim, live your healthiest life, and pray your child follows your example." I combine that message with the suggestion that parents offer children a "lifeline," a path back into the family fold, should they want one. Importantly, extending that lifeline should not mean that parents and other family members are victimized. It is better to do what is recommended when we see someone drowning: Stay safely on the bank and throw out a lifeline rather than jumping in and risking our own drowning.

of mental health and juvenile justice professionals. We usually advise parents against using radical, desperate acts of "tough love" designed to regain control and get kids to submit to parental authority. But calling the police or placing a child out of the home is sometimes a necessary strategy for preserving the safety and well-being of other family members. This is a defensive maneuver meant to be protective; it likely won't address the issues that brought about the harmful behaviors. Still, such actions convey to children, "I might not be able to control your behavior, but I can control mine. And I will act to keep from being your victim." Again, it's a defensive posture, not an offensive weapon. Parents should not abandon or reject children in a desperate effort to turn them around. If your child is placed out of the home, offer them a path back—a path that involves adhering to the minimal conditions that allow for everyone's safety.

LEARN THE SIX COMPONENTS OF AN ADAPTIVE CONTAINMENT SCRIPT

Disciplinary encounters with children who are defiant or disruptive can be stressful, emotionally charged events that leave parents feeling tired and full of doubt. Parents can better manage these events by adopting and using a behavioral script that's followed from start to finish. *Scripts* are overlearned action patterns performed in a rather automatic, consistent manner. A well-constructed containment script can help reduce the stress of disciplinary encounters and boost parents' confidence in their parenting. A containment script also ensures greater consistency in discipline: Parents are more likely to follow through to the end, and children will more readily learn what behaviors are allowed and what are not allowed. The best containment scripts are delivered calmly, firmly, and with a clear, quiet voice. Scripts help parents stay focused on the disciplinary goal without getting distracted by children's challenges and taunts. An adaptive containment script has the following features:

- seldom invoked
- consistently applied
- fully completed
- raises the cost of misbehavior
- feasibly used and reused
- nonviolent

Seldom Invoked (The "5-or-Fewer" Rule)

Because effective discipline is selective discipline, it helps if your list of disciplinary targets is short. We encourage parents to identify five or fewer behaviors that are important to children's growth and development and allow for an effective blend of acceptance and containment (see the Disciplinary Funnel in Figure 6.1). The 5-or-Fewer Rule is arbitrary, but it's a helpful way to ensure your containment script is not overused. The Disciplinary Funnel can be used to identify the level of target behaviors that should go on your short list to maintain a 4:1 ratio. As we noted earlier, active concerns about your child's use of coercion or aggression should certainly go on your short list of

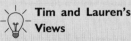

Tim and Lauren's Views

Tim: It's a "handy" rule: One target behavior per finger! Dad joke for the win!

Lauren: You can think of these behaviors as those that get you off the couch, no matter what.

disciplinary targets. If you don't have those concerns, then you might consider including one or two Do commands on your short list. Ideally, these are Do commands that have wide ripple effects. For example, the whole family benefits when children go to bed on time and obey household rules about where they can eat. By sticking to your short list of five or fewer target behaviors, you'll ensure that your containment script is seldom used, and you can better maintain a posture of acceptance.

Consistently Applied

Parents hear often about the importance of being consistent, especially with their discipline. Let's take a minute to unpack this oft-told piece of parenting advice. There are at least three types of parental consistency: verbal, interparental, and behavioral.

Verbal Consistency

Verbal consistency refers to those times when a parent gives a command or makes a request and then makes sure to follow through with that command. The underlying assumption is that there shouldn't be inconsistency between what a parent *says* and what they *do*. This could also be called *logical consistency*, in that it is logical to assume that what a parent says should be acted upon. For example, let's imagine Nevaeh has low grades and is at risk for being held back in school. Her mother is concerned and tells her daughter that anything less than a B– in math would mean Nevaeh loses her cell phone for 6 weeks. When the report card comes, Nevaeh has a C in math. If mom is determined to be consistent with what she says, then Nevaeh would go without her phone for 6 weeks. But a narrow use of logical consistency could mean missing other relevant factors, such as safety, convenience, or the developmental significance of the child's behavior. How critical is it that Nevaeh make a B in math? If Nevaeh doesn't have a phone, will she feel safe after school and will she be safe when waiting for a ride or walking home from a friend's house? Logical consistency also doesn't factor into a child's effort to meet parents' expectations. For example, what if Nevaeh had worked hard to raise her grade from a low F to a high C? Verbal consistency is tough to use, and it's not always needed or helpful. It's also the kind of consistency that can tie parents into knots, especially if they make hasty, ill-advised decisions and feel compelled to follow through with what they've said just to be consistent.

INTERPARENTAL CONSISTENCY

Interparental consistency is when parents and coparents agree on what children should or should not do. This is useful and can make life easier, but it's not essential unless the discrepancy between parents is large and meaningful. Sometimes big discrepancies signal underlying marital conflict, but most discrepancies are neither large nor meaningful. Grandma lets the kids eat ice cream before bedtime, but Dad doesn't; Mom lets the kids stay up late on Fridays when her partner is not around, but her partner gets them to bed early every night; Dad never gets fast food, but Tío Luca likes to get fast food when it's his night to "cook." These are minor discrepancies unlikely to have a negative impact on children. But inconsistencies can be problematic if one parent is undermining the other's authority. Imagine Grandma allowing the children to have ice cream after their father had told them to go to bed after their bath. If done routinely,

Dad's authority could be undermined, and his children will learn they can whine and get dessert. Inconsistency is also common and somewhat expected among parents who are separated or divorced. Rules and routines are likely to differ at each house, which can be annoying to the other parent but is seldom a significant risk for children's growth and development. More damaging is inconsistency and disagreements that result from the pain of divorce. When divorced parents put children in the middle psychologically, it is particularly damaging. Examples include parents who expect their children to be loyal to them and to keep secrets from the ex-spouse.

BEHAVIORAL CONSISTENCY

The most important form of parental consistency is *behavioral consistency*, which refers to consistency in how parents respond to a specific child behavior. For example, do parents consistently step in and set a limit when their child hits a sibling? Do they consistently let it slide when their child makes a rude comment? Behavioral consistency is exactly what we've been discussing with regard to selective discipline and using a short list of disciplinary targets. Behavioral consistency means consistently enforcing (100% of the time, remember?) the specific target behaviors on your short list. There might be two dozen troublesome or questionable behaviors performed by your son or daughter over a week's time, but your job is to be consistent in how you respond to the **specific behaviors on your short list**. We help our children when they can easily discriminate between behaviors that are allowed and not allowed. There's little risk to Nevaeh's mom changing her mind about taking the phone (given concerns about Nevaeh's safety and in acknowledgment of her academic effort) if Mom continues to communicate strong expectations about schoolwork and remains consistent in how she responds to the behaviors on her disciplinary short list. But imagine if Mom came home from work, had a drink to unwind, and was suddenly in a good mood. If she then let Nevaeh get away with things not typically allowed (e.g., push her brother, stay out past curfew), the inadvertent lesson being taught is not right from wrong but whether her mom is in a good or bad mood.

Fully Completed

Parents can feel defeated and spent from repeated disciplinary encounters, especially when children are prone to being irritable or demanding. And yet it's important to follow through with needed containment efforts, especially when the behavior in question is a key disciplinary target. The automatic, overlearned nature of containment scripts help parents persist toward an effective resolution to the disciplinary encounter, even when they are frustrated and weary and their children are defiant and angry.

Raises the Cost of Misbehavior

This point is tied to our earlier definition of effective discipline. There are several ways to determine if you've raised the cost of misbehavior. For young children whose ability to regulate emotions is not fully developed, raising the cost of their misbehavior is often signaled by crying, complaining, or screaming when firm limits are set. For older children and teens, the most obvious cue that you've effectively raised the cost of misbehavior is when your children stop engaging in the behavior or do so less often. But there are times when parents' efforts to set firm limits—to raise the cost of misbehavior—has no obvious, immediate impact. In fact, depending on how long children have been using the behavior and how reliably it has "worked" to get what they want, children could keep using it, almost as a test of parents' capacity to persist (also see our discussion of extinction bursts later in this chapter). Therefore, we recommend that parents persist in setting firm limits even when there's no immediate change in their child's behavior. This is particularly true when the disciplinary target is a serious behavior such as aggression or delinquency. We also encourage parents not to underestimate the costs of their disciplinary efforts and the likely impact over time. If parents can come close to 100% consistency in their efforts to set a limit on a given behavior, even if it appears to have little immediate impact, that is a costlier scenario for their child than not imposing a limit. Plus, your consistent efforts to set limits are an important part of conveying your expectations and values (see Chapter 7, "Lead").

Feasibly Used and Reused

Parenting a child with strong emotions and difficult behavior can be a lengthy, arduous process, and parents need to be equipped for the long haul. Some containment scripts carry a lot of punch but are not sustainable. For example, having children make amends for misdeeds and do additional chores can be a powerful but impractical approach to containment, especially if children frequently misbehave. A form of punishment that spans a long period of time, like Nevaeh's 6-week phone ban, can also be difficult to enforce repeatedly. These rather intensive strategies are also likely to be abandoned when parents are stressed or tired. The most useful containment scripts are those that can be used repeatedly and with minimal costs to parents. The costs to parents are usually determined by which sanction or form of punishment parents use. Later we discuss various options for sanctions and pay particular attention to the likely cost of parents using and reusing these options.

Nonviolent

Short of engaging in child abuse, parents have the freedom to choose how to discipline their child. In the United States, many parents report that they were spanked as a child and they "turned out okay." But the science is clear that physical punishment can lead to more, not less, childhood aggression, especially if it's intense and occurs in the absence of an accepting parent–child relationship. Children who are physically punished also tend to be more distrustful, more avoidant, and less responsive to parents than children whose parents do not use physical punishment. And yet it is not uncommon for parents, especially in the United States, to spank, swat, or use some other form of physical discipline.

Sometimes the use of physical discipline becomes abusive. Abusive parenting is often done impulsively, without a lot of deliberate thought. Indeed, it could be said that parents who act abusively are using a different kind of *disciplinary script*, one that shares many of the features of a healthy containment script (i.e., consistently applied, seldom invoked, fully completed, feasibly used and reused). Overlearned, automatic scripts for abusive parenting are often driven by angry feelings and hostile thoughts that are hard for parents to recognize and regulate. Unlike a healthy containment script, abusive disciplinary scripts are ill advised and damaging. Parents often turn to physical punishment when they're stressed or angry, which means that parents are modeling for children how to act when angry. In addition, discipline done when parents are highly emotional carries the risk of being heavy-handed. Yes, violent disciplinary scripts can sometimes bring children's misbehavior to a hard stop, but harsh parenting is rarely effective over time, even with children who are emotionally reactive and strong willed. Most importantly, the use of physical punishment is often a signal that discipline is less about helping children and more about helping parents' emotional distress.

BUILD A FOUR-STEP APPROACH TO CONTAINMENT

We offer here a simple, four-step approach to containment that can be used to build your own script. The first three steps—Instruct, Warn, and Sanction—should be familiar to most parents. With these three steps, children *learn* of your expectations for their behavior, *learn* about the consequences of not meeting those expectations, and *experience* the costs of failing to meet those expectations. The fourth and final step is probably least familiar. We call it Reconnecting. We use this term to describe a specific kind of parent–child interaction, one in which parents reaffirm their reasons for imposing a sanction while reminding children they are accepted and part of the family. This four-step approach is presented here along with other, potentially helpful options. Let's take a closer look at each step.

A Four-Step Approach to Containment

Basics

1. Instruct

Using a firm voice, state the expectation in a direct, clear, and specific manner. Use your facial expression, your posture, and your voice to make clear that you've now moved into "containment mode," focused and serious but not emotional and out of control.

- "Tanaz, we can't drive off until you buckle your seat belt."

2. Warn

If your child fails to follow the instruction, repeat it with a warning that lets your child know of the ensuing sanction.

- "Tanaz, if you don't buckle your seat belt, I'll have to leave you here with Grandma."

A Four-Step Approach to Containment (*Continued*)

3. Sanction

If your child fails to heed the warning, impose the sanction.

- "Tanaz, because you didn't buckle your seat belt, you're going to stay here with Grandma."

4. Reconnect

Later, when you're both settled emotionally, speak to your child and emphasize these three points: (a) your child is loved and accepted, (b) you are committed to enforcing this specific expectation, and (c) this expectation is a central part of your family's values.

- "Tanaz, I love you, and you're important to me and to this family. I can't let you ride in the car without a seat belt. It's too dangerous and against the law. That's not what we do in this family."

Options

Redirect your child to more appropriate behavior.

- "Tanaz, you don't have to like the seat belt, but you do need to wear it."

Reflect your child's comments, feelings, and desires.

- "Tanaz, I'm sorry you don't like using a seat belt."

Give your child a **reason** for the limit.

- "Tanaz, we're not safe when we ride in a car without a seat belt."

Reinforce your child's efforts in the case of Do instructions.

- "Tanaz, thank you for buckling your seat belt. Now we can all be safer."

Instruct

Research has shown that about half of the young children taken to a mental health clinic because of behavioral difficulties will obey their parents if given good instructions. To instruct means to state simply and clearly that a specific behavior is expected or that a specific behavior is not allowed. Without clear instructions, children can misunderstand and miss the fact that you're serious about the expectations. When parents use pained expressions, sad sighs, or repeated whines ("Will somebody in this house please help me?"), they are not giving children clear instructions. The best kind of instruction uses simple words, focuses on one behavior at a time, is developmentally appropriate (fits your child's age and abilities), and is stated in an assertive manner.

Imagine a mom who is asked to watch her neighbor's 4-year-old son (Cedric) for an hour, even though she's cooking dinner and supervising her own 8-year-old son (Len) and 9-year-old daughter (Nita). Now imagine that young Cedric stands absent-mindedly between Len and the TV. Mom looks in just as Len shoves Cedric out of the way. A simple instruction in this scenario might be, "Len, use your words if you want Cedric to move out of the way." It's clear and simple and helps get Len's attention because his name is used. The following examples are less specific and less effective: "Len!" "I saw that!" "What are you doing?!" "Don't make me come in there!" In addition to being clear and simple, it can help if your instructions are "packaged" in nonverbal cues that signal commitment to and seriousness about containment. We're referring here to being physically close, directly facing your child, making eye contact, speaking clearly and calmly and not yelling, and using a firm but nonthreatening tone.

Warn

A warning does two things. It reminds children of parents' expectations, and it gives notice of the sanction that will follow if the instruction is ignored. In the previous situation, Mom could warn

Len by saying, "Len, I've told you to use your words instead of pushing people. If you push Cedric again, you'll have no TV for the rest of the night." Sometimes a warning can help parents contain child misbehavior without using a sanction, which can benefit the parent–child relationship by avoiding the emotional weight of a potentially heated disciplinary conflict. Warnings are especially useful when used to guide children who are distractable, impulsive, or cognitively immature. Warnings can also be used to remind children of standing rules (e.g., "There is no hurting in this house" [The No Hurting Rule]). For example, in this scenario, instead of instructing Len not to push, Mom could have reminded him of the rule about not hurting others ("Len, remember the No Hurting Rule!") and warned him of an impending sanction if he pushes Cedric again.

There are also times when it's not a good idea to give a warning. For example, what if Len had aggressively kicked Cedric in the back? A push and a kick are both aggressive acts, but one is certainly more violent than the other. When the behavior is particularly violent and doesn't happen often (hopefully), it makes little sense to give a warning. Instead, it should be treated as a serious affront to what your family values ("We don't hurt others, Len"). Issuing a warning in these instances could result in Len learning that he's got one chance to really hurt someone before Mom intervenes.

Sanction

To sanction a child is to impose some sort of cost or penalty. A good instruction combined with a warning can reduce how often sanctions are needed but it won't eliminate completely the need for sanctions. There are four basic types of sanctions. The first two require little or no cooperation from children. The other two depend on children's cooperation and are harder to use. Each type of sanction has its advantages and disadvantages. In general, sanctions that require children's cooperation tend to be more effective than other sanctions. The four types are (a) physical discipline, (b) response cost, (c) time-out, and (d) overcorrection.

PHYSICAL DISCIPLINE

Physical discipline involves the use of spanking, physical restraint, or any other form of physical contact as punishment. As we noted earlier, many parents use physical discipline, especially with younger children. It has been estimated that 80% to 90% of adults in the United States were spanked as children (for a review, see Zolotor et al., 2008). However, rates of spanking are continually going down in the United States due to decreased parental approval. Recent estimates are that two thirds of parents now spank their children. In fact, research shows that *most* parents don't *want* to spank their children but tend to use it when agitated or angry, believing that other methods of discipline won't work. The fact that so many parents still use spanking is understandable when you consider that parents don't need help or cooperation from children to spank them and that it is a readily available form of punishment that can be used repeatedly.

The fact that a lot of parents choose to spank their children doesn't mean it's effective, and research doesn't show any real advantage when parents spank instead of using other sanctions. In fact, as children get older and bigger, most parents

Tim's View

When I work with parents who say they spank their children, I typically note the pros and cons of using different kinds of sanctions, including nonabusive physical discipline. However, I stand firm against parents' use of abusive spanking, given the scientific evidence against its value and because of my legal obligations as a mandated reporter of child abuse.

stop using it. There's a risk that spanking and other forms of physical discipline will be used too often or too intensely, bordering on or even becoming abusive parenting. Spanking is also a form of aggression, even at nonabusive levels, which makes rules about "no hurting" seem silly and hypocritical. We recognize

Lauren's View

There is evidence that even mild or infrequent spanking is associated with children's greater use of aggression with peers.

that spanking is a quick and easy way to let children know that certain misbehaviors will cost them. However, there's little evidence for the long-term benefits of spanking, but there is ample evidence showing that spanking can cause harm.

Problematic outcomes include increased risk of childhood depression and anxiety, substance use, physical health problems (e.g., heart disease, earlier death), poor school performance, and the likelihood of physical injury and emotional pain from the discipline itself. And don't forget that spanking typically doesn't guide children on *what to do*.

RESPONSE COST

Response cost is the name psychologists use for sanctions that involve taking something away from a child who misbehaves. The idea that a certain behavior or response comes with a cost is familiar to many parents. Taking away TV privileges, taking the car keys, docking an allowance, and grounding are all examples of

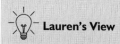

Lauren's View

Science has shown that parents can effectively discipline their children without resorting to the use of physical force. Therefore, it makes little sense to use an approach that models violence unless other, hidden goals are operating (e.g., what was modeled by parents, ease of use, emotion-based goals).

response cost. It happens to be one of the easiest sanctions to use. It doesn't take much effort *not* to drive your 14-year-old daughter to her friend's house because she didn't do her chores. It's easy to *not* give young children their favorite snack because they argued and hit each other. Of course, some children are very persistent and clever, so don't be surprised if they find ways to challenge or sidestep your attempts to use response cost. Many parents have learned this: They've learned to lock up video game controllers, unplug the TV, change the Wi-Fi password, or temporarily suspend cell phone service. And don't forget that some child misbehaviors have *natural* costs that help children learn right from wrong. For example, children who act mean or rude toward classmates are often excluded from group play; children who don't do their homework might miss going to recess.

The main challenge to using response cost is determining what is important or valuable enough to children that it would matter if it were taken away. If children have little adult supervision, abundant material possessions, and a weekly schedule full of fun activities, they might not be bothered by losing a single possession or a single privilege. But some privileges and possessions are especially valuable because they involve access to other things, like going to a friend's house, getting on social media, or texting their friends.

The other caution when using response cost is if the cost is too high or imposed too often. This can get in the way of parents being able to reuse the sanction. In the example of Len and Cedric, if Mom had said, "Len, no TV for a week," she couldn't easily use that same sanction the next day. Defiant children are seldom bothered by losing what's already lost, even if the period of loss is extended a few days. If you find that your child requires a sanction about once a week, then a 2- or 3-day response cost is workable. For younger children, taking something away for a single afternoon is likely sufficient. If your child's misbehavior occurs daily, then it's better to use a brief response cost period (e.g., "No TV for the rest of the day"), assuming, of course, the sanction carries sufficient costs to the child. We recommend erring in the direction of greater reusability than greater cost. That's because parenting a child with strong emotions and difficult behavior is a long-haul job, and heavy-handed sanctions could leave children feeling bankrupt and unloved, with nothing else to lose. If this were to persist over time, parents could be inadvertently sowing the seeds of dissatisfaction, discontent, and alienation. And there's little to be gained from pushing your child further away from you and your family.

TIME-OUT

One of the most widely recommended sanctions is time-out. Unlike response cost and physical discipline, time-out requires some level of child cooperation, which helps explain why it is perhaps recommended more than it's used. Effective use of time-out can be challenging, although it's probably more accurate to say that time-out can be hard to start using. Establishing time-out as a sanction means it's been used successfully at least once and can be reused when necessary. The term *time-out* is shorthand for time-out from reward or reinforcement. It refers to the fact that children placed in an isolated area, such as a chair in the corner or a small separate room, can't access the things and activities they would normally enjoy. This is important to remember if your plan for time-out involves having your child stay in a bedroom that has a TV, a computer, video games, and a phone.

Some parents find it difficult to place their child in time-out and walk away. They hang around, sometimes debating with upset children why they need to stay in time-out. For time-out to be effective, it's important for parents to walk away and for children to be on their own. Parents don't have to go far—simply turning away or going to the next room will do—but a child in time-out should be alone (even if monitored for safety). Unless children remain in time-out *on their own*, time-out never happened. When children remain in time-out of their own accord, they are showing signs of self-control.

It might not be for long and they might still be upset or angry, but the whole family is helped when children are able to remain in an assigned area when they could easily walk away. This is not true for all children and all families, but a child's learning to remain in time-out can be an important event in the history of the parent–child relationship. It signals that a child is now ready to defer to parents' authority. In this way, time-out is a two-for-one sanction: It raises the cost of misbehavior and helps instill in children a sense of containment.

Some parents view time-out as a chance for children to rest or calm down, like in a sporting event. It's not a bad idea for children who are highly emotional and spiraling out of control to go to their room or take a walk outside, but that's different from using time-out as a disciplinary sanction. Besides, children willing to take a voluntary time-out are probably not displaying a lot of problem behavior. It is not uncommon for parents to say they tried using time-out, but it didn't work. Often, though not always, time-out doesn't work when used incorrectly. In this chapter, we offer some recommended guidelines for using time-out. Before we discuss these guidelines, let's first address the age of children for whom time-out is appropriate. For young children between 2.5 and 6 years of age, time-out usually involves sitting in a chair designated as the time-out chair. Because young children have limited control over their big emotions, they might need to be carried to the time-out chair. For older children unwilling to sit in the time-out chair and for whom it's not appropriate to carry them, it's better to use a time-out room (see the recommended guidelines). Parents can be flexible with some aspects of time-out, but other aspects are essential, so it's helpful to review commonly recommended guidelines. If you're worried about using time-out in your home, consider consulting a licensed child and family therapist in your area. You can also access time-out guidelines on the Centers for Disease Control and Prevention website (https://www.cdc.gov/parents/).

Recommended Guidelines for Using Time-Out

Young Children (roughly ages 2.5–6 years)

1. **Sturdy chair:** Use a four-legged, study chair. Wooden dining room chairs are best. No swivel chairs, camping chairs, or rolling chairs.
2. **Boring corner:** Place the chair in a corner where the child can be watched but does not have distractions (a blank wall is best). Make sure the chair is far enough away from the wall so the child cannot kick the wall or touch anything near them.
3. **Putting your child in the chair:** If your child refuses to sit in the chair, pick up your child from behind (facing away from you, under the arms) and place them carefully into the chair.
4. **Walk away:** Tell your child clearly, firmly, but calmly that they are to stay in the chair until you tell them to get up. Do not continue speaking to the child. Walk away, don't look at the child (unless glancing to make sure they are safe), and remain quiet.
5. **Watch the clock:** A useful goal is to have your child sit in the chair for 3 minutes (or 1 minute for each year of their age).
6. **Ask if they are ready:** If time is up and your child has been quiet, even for a few seconds, ask if they are ready to get out of time-out (see the post–time-out guidelines).
7. **If they don't stay in the time-out chair:** If your child refuses to sit in the time-out chair, be ready with a backup plan. One option is to walk or carry your child to a safe "time-out room" that has few distractions (or remove distractions/breakable items). Have them stay in the room (you may need to hold the door) until they're ready to go back to the time-out chair. Another option is simply to walk or carry them back to the time-out chair as many times as needed until the child remains in the chair on their own for the full 3 minutes.

(continues)

Recommended Guidelines for Using Time-Out (*Continued*)

Older Children (usually ages 7 years and older)

1. **Safe room:** Find a room where there are few distractions or things that can be broken. Let your child know this room will be used as the "time-out room."
2. **Send your child to the room:** Tell your child to go to the "time-out room."
3. **Watch the clock:** A useful goal is for your child to stay in the room for 5 to 10 minutes (depending on their age).
4. **Ask if they are ready:** If time is up and your child is quiet and still in the room, ask if they are ready to get out of time-out (see the post–time-out guidelines).
5. **If they don't stay in the time-out room:** For older children, rather than holding the door to keep them in, identify three different privileges that can be taken away if they refuse to stay. If they open the door or leave before it is time, take away one privilege ("Because you opened the door before it was time, you cannot watch TV for the rest of the day. Stay in the room until I say you can come out"). Repeat this each time they try to leave the room. Time-out ends if all three privileges have been taken ("Because you didn't stay in your room, you lost TV time, going to your friend's house, and playing your game this evening. We will talk more about this tomorrow").

Time-out is not the right fit for all families. For example, children who were previously traumatized by severe neglect (e.g., long periods of time alone in a room with no supervision) should not be placed in a "time-out room." Also, the first time a parent uses time-out is usually the most difficult and can often take longer than any other time it's used. This is especially true if children aren't used to parents being firm and following through with a sanction. Their children could become very emotional and try lots of ways to resist going to time-out. This behavior is called an *extinction burst—*

a burst of more intense behavior (e.g., yelling, hitting, running away) that occurs when a less intense behavior (e.g., whining) is no longer "working." Such is the case when parents suddenly "extinguish" (i.e., stop rewarding) a behavior that had been used previously by children. It helps to know about extinction bursts beforehand, so you can be mentally prepared for these strong reactions when they happen.

Post–Time-Out Guidelines. If you're worried that time-out has gone on too long, or if you're feeling drained by the emotional costs of time-out, you can choose to end it by taking away a privilege. Just remember, you decide when time-out is over, not your child. Finally, it's important to *reconnect* with your child when time-out is over and you're both calm (discussed later in this chapter). Remind your child that they are loved and accepted, that you are committed to enforcing certain expectations, and that those expectations are important to the family ("I love you, but I can't allow that

 Lauren's View

When setting firm boundaries, I remind parents that there will likely be pushback from children, especially if they are used to getting away with certain behaviors. Pushback can involve both verbal coercion ("I hate you! You're the worst parent ever!") and physical aggression (kicking, biting, or screaming), especially with younger children. I often ask parents of young children what is the worst thing their children have ever said or done to them. I then predict they're likely to see it again when they first set firm limits on children's misbehavior. It helps to know that problem behavior can often get worse before it gets better. But once a firm limit has been set and parents have not given in, then problem behavior tends to quickly decrease in frequency. So, stay the course!

behavior. It's not what we do in this family"). It can also help to go over the time-out procedure with your children before using it. State your expectations clearly, show them what will happen when they are in time-out, and let them know you will tell them when time-out is over.

Time-Out Hints. If you decide to start using time-out, here are some additional helpful hints:

- We suggest you *not* start using time-out unless you have time to devote to it. For some strong-willed children, that could mean 30 minutes or 3 hours.
- Make sure you're rested and in a good mood before forging ahead.
- If you have a coparent, schedule initial attempts at time-out when your partner is there to lend emotional support. Don't ask your partner to help physically because the goal is for *you* to contain *your* child.
- Recognize there will likely be some messiness: Your child might not like time-out, they might not like you, and you might not like them! You might get tired of having to walk them back to time-out. You might not like them pulling out all the stops to get you to give in and end time-out early. And we can almost guarantee that you won't like it if they wet themselves, throw up on you, wipe snot on your walls, or call you nasty names. By the time you're done, you might be worn out physically and emotionally. But know that once you've established time-out and your children know that you're committed to using it, it becomes a lot easier to use.

OVERCORRECTION

Like time-out, overcorrection is well supported by science and requires your child's cooperation. *Overcorrection* is a sanction that involves having children do a specific task designed to correct their misdeed. In fact, *correcting work* might be a more accurate label for this sanction. The *over* part of overcorrection refers to the practice of having children do *more* than is needed to correct their misdeed. For example, a child who punches a hole in a wall might be given the job of repairing the hole *and* painting all the walls in the room. When the misdeed involves hurting another person, parents must be more creative when using overcorrection. For example, a boy who kicks his sister might be required to do her chores *and* to write her a note of apology. The chief advantage to using overcorrection is that children are required to do something positive. Overcorrection also gives parents a chance to actively guide their children as they do these good works. By helping children in this way, parents can forge a working partnership that could add significantly to children's sense of belonging. The most obvious disadvantage to overcorrection is that children might refuse to do the work, which could mean having a backup sanction (e.g., taking away a privilege) to ensure children do the assigned work.

Reconnect

It's important that children know their parents can restrict their behavior when it's necessary, but it's also important that discipline is not so harsh or heavy that children withdraw emotionally and psychologically. Parents can usually sense when a child is growing distant from the family. It's especially important to track whether a child is becoming alienated from or is actively rejecting their family and its values. One way to prevent a slide toward alienation is to take time *after* a disciplinary encounter to reconnect with your children. Reconnecting interactions can be used to clarify the message of restraint behind any imposed sanctions and correct any misinterpretations your children have about their sense of place in the family. More importantly, postpunishment reconnecting serves to repair emotional damage to the parent–child relationship that might have occurred. To reconnect after the disciplinary dust has settled is to bring children back into the fold of the family.

To help you picture what it means to reconnect with your children, let's go back to the example of 8-year-old Len, the boy who pushed his 4-year-old neighbor, Cedric. Imagine that Mom put Len in time-out for his misdeed. Once he's done with time-out, she can now look for a chance to have a brief, reconnecting visit with him. If he were to go right back to watching TV or if he's still angry about being placed in time-out, then she should wait before attempting to reconnect. Once they're both ready and available, Mom can reconnect using a three-part message. First, Len is accepted. Second, Mom is committed to containing his aggressive behavior. Third, aggression is not in keeping with the values and beliefs of their family. Here's an example of how this might be said:

> Len, I know you didn't like being in time-out. I don't like putting you there. I love you and you are important to me and to this family. But I'm not going to let you hurt others. Each time you push or hit, I'll put you right back in time-out. In our family, we don't hurt other people.

In this simple message, Len's mother touches on all three core conditions of a healthy parent–child relationship—Accept, Contain, and Lead.

Useful Containment Options

The basic four-step approach to containment described earlier can be augmented at times with the following options: redirecting, reflecting, reasoning, or reinforcing. These options don't work every time for every kid, but all are worth considering.

REDIRECTING

Redirecting is the technique of combining an instruction with a description of what is permitted. For example, Len's mother could have said, "Len, don't push Cedric. If he's in the way, use your words and ask him to move."

REFLECTING

Reflecting refers to the use of reflective listening to let children know that you understand and accept their feelings, even though you're standing firm on their behavior. For example, Len's mother might say, "Len, I know you're mad that Cedric is at our house and is getting in the way, but you can't hurt him just because you're mad." The ability to restrict children's misbehavior while simultaneously accepting their negative feelings is a very handy skill for parents. Too many parents consider negative emotions as part of the overall package of "bad behavior." When you reflect children's feelings while standing firm on misbehavior, you *uncouple* feelings from behavior. You don't have to choose between validating your children's feelings (but giving in to bad behavior) *or* being firm on misbehavior (but ignoring feelings). You can accept their feelings *and* contain their misbehavior.

REASONING

Reasoning refers to parents explaining to children why they are being disciplined. Reasoning can sometimes help children be more cooperative, but it's mainly used to clarify your expectations. For example, Len could have been told, "Cedric is only 4 years old and doesn't realize when he's in the way. So be easy on him." Of course, reasoning can be counterproductive when children are simply debating parents' use of a sanction because they don't like it or agree with it.

REINFORCING

Reinforcing refers to the use of praise or other forms of reward when children use behaviors that are positive, acceptable alternatives to what's been restricted. For example, if Len sat on the floor by Cedric or invited Cedric to join him on the couch, that would be a great opportunity for Mom to say, "Why, Len! That's nice of you to let Cedric sit with you! Now, both of you can see the TV." Reinforcing is particularly useful when your expectations involve children doing things that are new, difficult, or challenging. Reinforcing is also a great way to make clear the distinction between behaviors that are positive and allowed (sharing, using words) and behaviors that aren't allowed (hitting, pushing).

BUILDING YOUR OWN CONTAINMENT SCRIPT

A four-step approach to containment can form the foundation for your own containment script. If you successfully apply all four steps (Instruct, Warn, Sanction, and Reconnect), you'll have a greater chance of promoting your child's sense of containment. You will also be more likely to limit negative emotional exchanges, restrict serious misbehavior, and avoid being a victim of your children's coercion. Clear instructions and timely warnings can solve lots of disciplinary concerns, so use them well. And if you're trying to contain an unruly, strong-willed child, a key feature of your script will be your choice of sanctions. Keep in mind the advantages and disadvantages of each type of sanction. Remember also to follow disciplinary conflicts with a reconnecting interaction, giving you a chance to touch base with your children and bring them back into the family fold.

CONTAIN HOMEWORK

Once you have identified your short list of specific disciplinary targets and built your new containment script, all that's left is to practice using it. Only through repeated practice can your new script begin to feel comfortable, automatic, and useful. Practice can include the following:

- Narrow your disciplinary focus by using the Disciplinary Funnel to create your short list of specific disciplinary targets or expectations.
- Keep in mind the fixed-ratio system as you track how often interactions with your child are positive/neutral (80%) or negative (20%).
- Use the four-step approach (Instruct, Warn, Sanction, and Reconnect) to construct and use an adaptive containment script that has these six features:
  - seldom invoked
  - consistently applied
  - fully completed
  - raises the cost of misbehavior
  - feasibly used and reused
  - nonviolent

CHAPTER 7

LEAD: WOULD YOU FOLLOW YOU?

Effective leaders have an ability to get along with others while holding tight to their beliefs and values. When leaders blend strong convictions with harmonious relationships, they inspire others, serve others, and draw others to them. As a parent, it's your task to lead your family. Leading is the third and final condition for a strong, healthy parent–child relationship and a critical aspect of our holistic, long-term model of parenting. The interconnections among these three conditions (Accept, Contain, and Lead) are most apparent when it comes to leading. That's because leading is both (a) a necessary complement to accepting and containing and (b) a result of combining a posture of acceptance *with* an effective, selective discipline strategy. When you can maintain both harmony *and* order in your home, when children obey you *and* enjoy being with you, you *are* their leader. There are other things you can do to enhance your role as family leader (and there are things you can do to detract from that role), but there's no better foundation for leading than the combination of accepting with containing.

This chapter aims to help you

- learn to lead by serving the greater good;
- learn to lead by giving voice to important lessons and core values;

- learn to use the Third Option;
- lead by being a healthy, worthy example; and
- recognize four key obstacles to leading.

LEADING IN CONTEXT

Children play an active role in their own development; they are not empty buckets into which we drop pearls of wisdom or mere blank slates upon which we write their life story. Children make choices, especially as they get older and choose where and with whom they spend time. They might turn and follow us, or they might spend time elsewhere. Sometimes they look up to us, sometimes they don't. They might think of us with pride or alternatively, disappointment. Some children admire and respect their parents; others have little or no respect for the adults in their home. As parents, we can't control what's in our children's hearts and minds. We can't insist they love us. We can't make them respect us. We can't make them believe all that we believe or value all that we value. But they are watching us, and they see what makes sense and what doesn't add up. Over time, they draw their own conclusions about what's real and what's fake about our lives.

Servant-Leaders

In 1970, Robert K. Greenleaf, a retired AT&T executive, published an essay titled "The Servant as Leader." He wanted folks to rethink what it means to lead. For Greenleaf, *servant-leaders* don't simply *want* to serve; they want *first* to serve. For them, leading is an after-thought, not a first thought. But what does that have to do with parenting? We would suggest quite a lot. Consider how Greenleaf described a "good test" of whether someone is a servant leader: Do those served grow as persons? Do they, *while being served*, become healthier, wiser, freer, more autonomous, and more likely to become servants themselves?

To help you picture what it means for parents to lead, we suggest this image: Parents lead their family when they *carry* things. And there are three main things to carry.

CARRY THE WATER: SERVING THE GREATER GOOD

The expression "carry the water" means serving others or doing things to help others. For parents, this generally means making decisions that benefit the whole family or doing tasks that perhaps no one else can do or wants to do. As servant-leaders, parents handle important but unpleasant tasks. Examples include the following:

- making difficult decisions (that please no one);
- making important choices (e.g., about money and spending);
- making plans (e.g., for dinner, for holidays, for trips);
- doing little jobs each day that keep family members clothed, fed, and housed; and
- paying attention to what other family members want or need.

This list is also a good reminder that parents must attend to their own health and well-being, if they are to lead. For leaders, self-care is a necessity—not a luxury.

CARRY THE MESSAGE: GIVING VOICE TO IMPORTANT LESSONS AND VALUES

We use the phrase "carry the message" as a reminder that children are looking for answers to important questions in life. Many of these questions are answered by knowing and embracing what their parents value and believe. Thus, it's important that parents not hide these away in their heart but share them openly and often.

There are lots of ways parents can do that, including preaching, teaching, storytelling, praising, praying, speaking out, and showing up. Some parents downplay their role as teachers, as opinion leaders, or as givers of values. They assume their child already knows what they value and believe, or they assume someone else will be teaching their child these important life lessons. Here are some of the big questions for which children seek answers:

- School and academics
  - What kind of grades are expected of me?
  - How do I deal with teachers who I don't like?
  - How much school do I need?
- Use of tobacco, alcohol, or drugs
  - Are these dangerous or not?
  - My parents drink (or smoke). Can I?
  - My friends drink (or smoke). Can I?
  - I'm too young to get addicted, right?
- Friends and peers
  - Will other kids like me? Will I be popular?
  - Will I have a best friend?
  - What if other kids don't like me or bully me?
  - How should I treat kids who are different than me?
  - What's the big deal about peer pressure?
- Dating and sex
  - What if I'm confused or scared about sex?
  - Will someone ever want to date me?
  - What are my beliefs about having sex?
  - My friends are having sex. Should I?
- Money and career
  - Are we rich or are we poor?
  - Do I need to know about managing money?
  - How do I choose a job or a career?

- Identity, race and ethnicity, and culture
  - Am I proud of my race and ethnicity and my culture? How should I show it?
  - What does our family believe about faith or religion?
  - What if people mistreat me because of the color of my skin?
  - Will my parents and family love me if I'm gay, bisexual, gender nonconforming, or transgender?
  - Who am I, really? What is my true self? How can I express who I am?

Children answer many of these questions by living with and getting to know their parents. Much is revealed by how parents act and what children see and hear. This is what it means for parents to carry the message of values and beliefs. Children learn by how we treat others, by how we react to what's said about their friends or other kids at school, by our responses to things they say and do, and by the opinions we share when talking about various topics over dinner. But

 Lauren's View

In my work with families of children who have experienced trauma such as sexual abuse, I often teach parents about the importance of speaking openly with their child about appropriate sexual behavior, personal space, and safety precautions. Some don't want to have these conversations because doing so makes them uncomfortable. They fear these conversations will hurt their child, or they believe their child is too young to have these conversations. But for children who have been sexually abused, the message they've received about their body and about sex was delivered in ways that were exploitive and harmful. They need to hear from parents a different, better, healthier message so they can make sense of what they experienced. These difficult conversations can also be preventative: Research shows that abusive adults are less likely to victimize children who learn about personal space and are taught the names of their private parts.

some children need more from their parents; they need a message that is clear, loud, and leaves no doubt about what parents believe. For example, teens who come into this world with a difficult, challenging temperament and a tendency to be impulsive show a tendency to dismiss parents' beliefs about things that are risky but appealing (e.g., drinking, smoking). In fact, unless their parents deliver a very clear, abstinence-based message about drinking, these higher risk teens are likely to think parents are okay with their use of alcohol.

There are, of course, some parents who lean in the other direction: They overteach and underlisten. Children will hear their parents when they feel heard by their parents. Parents who preach but don't listen, who teach but never learn, will undercut their own positive message. So, the best way to "carry" a message about important life lessons and core values is through the parent–child relationship. In fact, when you package your message in a relationship that blends acceptance and containment, you speak volumes, even when you speak softly.

CARRY YOURSELF: LEADING BY EXAMPLE

According to Webster's dictionary, the word "carry" can also mean to hold or comport oneself in a specific manner. We use it here to refer to parents who lead by being a worthy example, someone children admire, respect, and follow. The famous saying, "Be the change you want to see in the world," often attributed to Gandhi, is another way to think about this way of leading your family. Parents who lead are those who care about the example they set for their children. Every conversation, every interaction with a non-family member, every disappointment endured, and every task set before them is a potential lesson for their children. On the other hand, parents who spend lots of time complaining, blaming, and failing are not carrying themselves well and thus are less likely to be admired, respected, and followed.

Research on modeling—the process of learning by watching others—tells us that children tend to imitate the behavior of powerful adults and tend to tune out or dismiss the behavior of adults they view as powerless. Parents can use this information to be a more compelling example for their children. Especially helpful is when parents blend a consistent message of belonging with a narrow message of restraint. It's a strategy that speaks to parents' role as the family leader: "I take care to manage my own emotions and behavior and I will, if I need to, step in to manage your behavior." Children also make judgments about parents based on their health and well-being, on the extent to which they maintain clear generational boundaries, on how they treat others, on what they value and achieve, and on what is said about their parents in the community. All of this information is pooled to make up what is colloquially known as how parents carry themselves in the eyes of their children. Think of it as an index of respect and admiration (or disrespect and derision). The higher the "score," the more likely it is that children will follow parents' example.

THE THIRD OPTION

There are several options for leading your children and your family. Your first option, *acceptance*, is a message of belonging and tolerance; sometimes it's even a message of affirmation, admiration, or approval. Your children are not only free to act a certain way, but they also see and hear you cheering them on. Your second option, *containment*, is a message of restraint and intolerance. Your children see you step in and stand firm on certain issues, even if it means conflict and unpleasant feelings. Accepting and containing offer very different options when deciding how to respond to children's behavior. You see your 6-year-old daughter taking peanut butter from her sandwich and using it as "lipstick," much to the amusement of her younger sister. You feel the urge to intervene, but you decide to wait and see if she eventually eats her sandwich. You choose acceptance. You see your 11-year-old son grab his little brother, rip the TV remote from his hands, and change the channel even though the little brother had been watching his favorite cartoon show. You see this as an act of physical aggression, so you step in with a sanction for the older brother. You choose containment. But accepting and containing are not your only options in every situation; you have a third option.

Imagine a dad sitting with his 10-year-old son. Lately, his son has been teasing his 8-year-old sister about an embarrassing incident that involved her friends. She was drinking milk in the school cafeteria when she suddenly laughed, and milk spewed out through her mouth and nose. It was truly funny, and everyone laughed, including the little sister. But now her brother's constant reminders of the incident seem to hurt her feelings. She might need support from her dad to help deal with her brother's teasing, but right now Dad has a chance to say something to her brother. What should he say? Should he issue a warning ("Hey, stop teasing your sister. If you do it again, you'll be punished") or impose a sanction ("You've been mean to your sister, so I've decided there's no TV for you tonight")? Both are a bit much, especially if his son doesn't realize the impact of his actions.

A better option in this situation, *one that's neither accepting nor containing*, is what we call the Third Option. You'll notice in Figure 7.1 that to Lead is to act in a way that is between choosing to Accept or Contain. It is neither accepting nor containing. That's the essence of the Third Option—leading children in those in-between situations that are not a good fit for either accepting or containing.

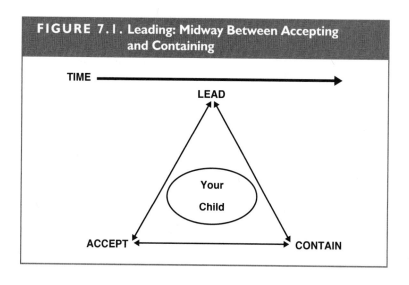

FIGURE 7.1. Leading: Midway Between Accepting and Containing

In this scenario, Dad's use of the Third Option might sound like this: "That thing with your sister and the milk was pretty funny, but I think your comments are starting to hurt her feelings, which is not so funny."

Let's take a closer look at this third option. It has three parts, and all are important if you're going to use it. The *first* is a simple description of your child's behavior (and perhaps acknowledgment of emotion expressed). This should be neither accusatory nor critical; instead, it should sound like a reporter offering a neutral description of what was seen and heard (e.g., "I noticed that you mentioned again that funny story about your sister and the milk"). The *second* part is a reminder of what your family believes and values (e.g., "We care about one another and try not to hurt each other"). When these two things—an observation of your child's behavior/emotions and your family's values—are placed side by side in the same comment, it creates for children a kind of gentle feedback. It's a helpful, supportive message that says, "Here's what I noticed you doing and here's what we believe. You do the math."

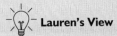

Lauren's View

Of course, younger children can't "do the math," so they need greater values-based messages that are clear and direct. For toddlers or preschoolers, you might need to ask questions such as, "What do we do if we've hurt someone's feelings?" I remind my young children how their actions and words can make others feel ("You helped that girl when she fell down. I bet that helped her feel better," "I know you're mad, but when you yelled at him and said you never wanted to play with him again, I think that really hurt his feelings"). Sometimes I give specific instructions on how to act in a values-based way ("I think it might help if you apologized and offered a hug") or offer suggestions about values-based behavior ("Let's see if we can all be friends. Let's say what our favorite thing is about each other. I'll go first!").

The *last* and perhaps most important part of the Third Option is the *period*, the little dot at the end that says, "That's all." It carries an implicit message that if voiced would sound like this:

> I'm not saying that you're in trouble for what you've been doing, but I'm also not saying that I approve of what you're doing. I'll leave it to you to decide what happens next, but I thought you should have the feedback.

Putting in that period and stopping—saying nothing else—is probably the hardest part of using the Third Option. Parents who do well with the first two parts will have to fight the urge to keep going. They might feel a pull to keep preaching or teaching, wanting to "make sure" their children "fully understand" or "really get the message." Parents who don't stop at the period, who go past it and say more, are trying to manage the uncertainty and discomfort that comes with allowing this situation to play out on its own. They want assurance that a particular outcome (e.g., their child doing the "right" thing) is going to happen. So, when parents use the Third Option and stop at the period, they are tolerating a certain level of ambiguity and discomfort. They won't know exactly how things will shake out. So, stopping at the period is the biggest challenge of using the Third Option.

Let's consider another example. Imagine that your 15-year-old daughter has a boyfriend named Derrick. This is her first serious dating relationship, and you think Derrick *might* be a good guy but you're not sure. You insisted on meeting Derrick before she could date him, but you still don't know him very well. When he comes to your home, he hardly speaks and doesn't look you in the eye. Derrick's older brother recently got arrested for selling drugs, and you wonder if Derrick is also involved with drugs. You don't know that; you only have your suspicions, your biases, and your worries. You do know that he's 17 years old and he smokes cigarettes, which is illegal and not a good fit with your family's values and beliefs. Here's how the Third Option might sound in this situation:

> *You:* Hi, honey. Got a minute? I've been thinking about you and Derrick.
>
> *Daughter:* Why? What's wrong? I bet you think he's a stoner just because of how he looks. I knew you were going to do this.
>
> *You:* Whoa! Hang on. You knew I was going to do what?
>
> *Daughter:* Make me stop seeing him.
>
> *You:* Because I think he uses drugs?
>
> *Daughter:* Yeah.
>
> *You:* Well, I don't know that he uses drugs. Does he use drugs?
>
> *Daughter:* No, but you think he does.

You: Well, honey, you're right. I don't know that he uses drugs.

Daughter: So what's the problem?

You: Well, that's a good question. I don't know if there is a problem. I know that Derrick smokes cigarettes, which at his age is against the law. It's also not something I'd want you to do. None of us smoke because it's harmful.

Daughter: Well that's not me. I don't smoke and I don't think his smoking is anybody else's business.

You: You're right. It is his choice. And if he wasn't dating my daughter, I wouldn't say anything. But he *is* dating my daughter and she's around him, a lot. And she really likes him. I see that smile on your face when he calls or comes by. Yes, it is his choice to smoke, to break the law and to do something unhealthy, but these aren't choices I like or that I agree with.

Daughter: And?

You: And what?

Daughter: Is that it?

You: That's it.

This exchange is a nice illustration of how the Third Option is neither accepting nor containing but a strategy that falls somewhere in the middle. There is no attempt to limit the daughter's behavior, but there's also no doubt that her parent has concerns about Derrick and his smoking. And this parent does a good job of stopping after sharing their observation about Derrick's smoking and how that sits outside their family's values.

A critical component of using the Third Option is having confidence in what you know and believe and having the courage to say what you know and believe. What you know is what you've seen and what you believe is what your family values. A quick way to try out the Third Option is to use this formula: "I see you doing X. We believe Y." Notice also how the mom in this example readily conceded what she *didn't* know—whether Derrick uses drugs. Still, she was steadfast in stating what she did know (i.e., Derrick smokes cigarettes and smoking is illegal for someone his age) and what she believed (smoking is unhealthy and potentially harmful).

Of course, parents being aware of what they know is not the same thing as parents being *right* about what they know. It's better to view the Third Option as gentle, caring feedback designed to serve and support your child. It's a way to use love and wisdom to lead. The *quality* of your message will depend on your willingness to speak to what you know, to admit to what you don't know, and to stop at the period. The *power* of your message, whether it benefits your children, will depend on the quality of your relationship. Your honest and caring observations, coupled with simple reminders of shared family beliefs and values, can be quite compelling when children have a sense of belonging and are reliably but narrowly contained.

A Caution

There are times when parents should be cautious about using the Third Option. It should never be used to show that your views are correct and that your child's views are wrong. It's also not a time for bringing into your relationship rumors or other forms of vague information told to you by others. You can quickly lose credibility and respect when you cling too strongly to your own opinions or rely on the opinions of others. The Third Option is also a poor fit for parent–child relationships that are feeling the weight of harsh words, hurt feelings, and little or no communication for several weeks.

When the Third Option is used in that kind of relationship, there's a good chance it'll be heard as a lame lecture from someone who doesn't have a clue. The problem isn't the quality of the message—it's the quality of the relationship.

Parents should also be cautious about using the Third Option with younger children. As a form of gentle feedback, the Third Option is useful for in-between situations, but it's also a rather nuanced message that could leave younger children feeling confused or accused. As children grow older (school age and up) and begin to express their opinions more openly, the Third Option takes on increased utility. Older children usually wish to feel heard, and you probably want to hear them . . . up to a point. Keeping open lines of communication is important but you'd also like those lines of communication to go both ways, at least every now and then. It can be frustrating when we don't feel heard. But the answer is not talking more; it's talking less, listening more, listening deeply, and listening sincerely. If your relationship with your child lacks positive two-way communications, do the relationship work of spending time with your children, without an agenda, combining reflective listening with limited talking.

At the same time, hang tight to your family's values and beliefs. Don't compromise on that which is core to you and your family, even if your child is not buying it. This is where a healthy parent–child relationship, especially a posture of

Lauren's View

When setting a limit with my young children, I often notice they continue to ask "why" or repeat a question when they don't like my answer (or even run to my husband to see if he will give them what they want after I say "no"). It is easy to get frustrated that they aren't just listening, but I've also found that going back and forth and trying to make them understand how frustrated I am doesn't make things better either (for me or them).

acceptance, buys you so much. Parents need a strong foundation when taking an unpopular stand and a healthy parent–child relationship is that foundation. Nurture it, work hard to maintain it, and don't be afraid to use it when your defiant, disrespectful child has you nearly convinced that you're the world's worst parent and an all-time idiot. Some parents don't believe their relationship is a resource. They doubt the power and leverage that comes from a good relationship with their children. Instead of trusting that the relationship can withstand pushback when standing firm, these parents give in. Ironically, they give in to *save* the relationship, but instead they're likely to lose twice. These parents lose once when their child gets away with misbehavior, and they lose again when their child no longer respects them because they caved under pressure. When you unwisely give in to save the parent–child relationship, you risk causing the relationship to implode. Keep in mind the expression the Navajo use when someone is behaving badly, "He acts as if he has no relatives." Despite what your sons and daughters might say, they don't want to be without family or without you. Nurture, trust, and use your relationship to lead your child.

A common scenario for using the Third Option is when children start to encounter things that are unfamiliar or new. Perhaps they are meeting people who are different (e.g., don't fit certain gender or racial stereotypes), earning their own spending money, making choices about how to dress or wear their hair, learning divergent views on religion or politics, or encountering shifting attitudes among peers about sex or alcohol. For example, imagine that your 13-year-old son announces plans to get his septum pierced (like a bull ring), that your 17-year-old is working and saving money to buy a motorcycle, or that your 7-year-old has been teasing a boy at school for having long hair. These are excellent opportunities to use the Third Option. Remember, it has three parts: (a) what you've observed, (b) what your family values or believes, and (c) the period at the end, which is your signal to stop. Consider the following examples of what you might say:

- I don't know many people with septum piercings, but I do know that if piercings aren't washed properly, they can get infected, swell, and sometimes cause scarring. I am happy to support your personal expression, and I want you to do it wisely.
- I see that you're excited about getting a motorcycle and that you're working hard to make that happen. I'll be honest, motorcycles scare me, and I worry about your safety, which is important to me. I've known people who had serious injuries from motorcycle wrecks. I know you're careful, but not everyone is as careful as you.
- I heard you teasing that boy with long hair. In our family, we don't tease others for how they look or dress. We believe everyone is free to choose how they look or dress.

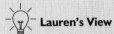

Lauren's View

Remember, certain forms of expression don't change who your child is. Black hair and clothes don't make your child a worse student. Piercings and tattoos don't make your child a delinquent. But comments from parents that are rejecting, sarcastic, or hurtful can harm children more than a change in their appearance. Be careful about going to battle over things that are not comfortable or "normal" to you. Remember the key signs of healthy growth and development that were discussed in Chapter 2 ("Goals"): relatedness, autonomy, and competence.

Another timely use of the Third Option is when you set a limit or impose a sanction and it's not sitting well with your child. Let's extend the earlier example of Derrick, the boy who is dating your 15-year-old daughter. Imagine that you just grounded your daughter and took her phone for the rest of the weekend because she got home late from a Friday night date. Pay close attention to what is said and done in this example. Note also that we used language that is probably milder than that used in many other families!

Daughter: Mom! I can't believe you're grounding me.

You: I know. But I was clear on when you needed to be home.

Daughter: It's so stupid. I mean, I got home 10 minutes late and you ground me for the whole freaking weekend. I don't get that.

You: I know you don't think it's fair, but that's what we're doing.

Daughter: But why?! I mean, do you really think 10 minutes is that big a deal?! Seriously, what did you think we were doing in our "10 minutes"?

You: I don't know, honey. I just know we agreed that you'd be home by 11 p.m.

Daughter: Can I at least have my phone?! That's so unfair. You're doing that just because you don't like Derrick. You think he's this big druggie. It's so lame!

You: [*Pause. Take a deep breath. Look at your daughter. Say nothing.*]

Daughter: I mean, it's not like I can't talk to him. We can still send messages online. So, your little plan to keep us apart won't even work. It's stupid!

You: It might be stupid, but I was clear on what time you needed to be home. And you're right; it does seem silly to take your phone if you can still send messages online, but that's the way it is.

Daughter: But why? It won't even work! What do you honestly think you'll get out of this? Do you really think I'll quit dating Derrick? Do you really think your little punishment will matter?

You: I'm not trying to stop you from seeing Derrick. I just know that you got home after curfew and that we take that seriously in our family.

Daughter: That is such a load of crap! Why don't you say what you really think: You hate the fact that I'm dating Derrick and you've been waiting for a chance to bust me so you can keep us apart.

You: Do you really believe that?

Daughter: Yes!

You: Well, you're right that I'm not a huge Derrick fan. I really don't like the fact that he smokes cigarettes. But I am not doing this to keep you two apart. You like Derrick and I see that you enjoy spending time with him. It might not make sense to me, but I love you and I want you to have room in your life to make your own choices. I'll step in if I think you're not safe, but that's not what's going on here. I'm just letting you know that you don't have a free pass when it comes to the curfew.

There's a lot happening in this conversation, and a lot a parent could chase—unproductively. But standing firm on the sanction and using the Third Option is a helpful combination. This example illustrates how you can be honest with your observations and true to your values: You admit to what you don't know, but you're clear about what you do know and believe. Consider also what you're not chasing, what you're not debating: your daughter's cursing, accusations, attitude, rhetorical questions, and predictions that your sanction is silly and won't work. Perhaps the most important thing you aren't chasing are self-doubts when trying to be a firm but caring mom. You make room for self-doubt and ambiguity ("What if I'm making a mistake?"), you make room for anger and hurt ("I didn't deserve that comment!"), and you make room for fear ("I don't want to lose my daughter!"), but you stand firm. It is tempting for parents to defend and justify their sanctions, hoping they can avoid unpleasant emotions. But being the leader of the family means managing and making room for difficult emotions so you can prioritize your child's growth and development.

FOUR OBSTACLES TO LEADING

Several factors could make it hard for parents to be a positive leader in their family. Next, we discuss four main obstacles to leading.

Parents Have Values That Are Unusual or Aberrant

Few parents hold beliefs that are clearly deviant or antisocial, but it is not uncommon for parents to endorse actions that some might consider troublesome. For example, some parents tell their children not to let others hurt or take advantage of them; however, some parents go further and coach their children to respond aggressively when treated badly (e.g., "I want you to hit back if somebody is teasing or starting trouble"). This kind of advice could also be misinterpreted, with children "hearing" that parents believe it's okay to hit anyone who disrespects them. Another example is when children are told that they should only listen to and obey their parents—not the teachers at school and not any other adults. Sometimes this advice comes from parents who have experienced firsthand the hurt

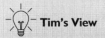

of exploitive adults or the pain of oppression and racial prejudice.

Parents Are Caught in an Unhealthy Lifestyle

We occasionally work with parents who struggle with difficult life circumstances: homelessness, poverty, domestic violence, chemical dependency, or mental illness. Our experience tells us these parents generally hold to the same positive, prosocial values of many other parents. There was also likely a time in their life when they lived out those values. Yes, now they might be susceptible to unhealthy, maladaptive, or even antisocial patterns of behavior, but rarely are these parents openly hostile or antisocial in their interactions with others, including their children. In fact, we have worked with many parents who are dedicated to ensuring their children have more opportunities than they had and none of the trauma they experienced as children. Still, some parents are living under very trying circumstances for child-rearing. They are isolated and underresourced and lack a sense of community that can support them and a system of shared prosocial beliefs. There are also some parents who fall prey to deviant lifestyles (use of illicit drugs, robbery, money fraud, sex trafficking) because of abusive, antisocial partners or because they struggle with serious mental illness or substance use. Not all is lost for these parents, but it can be quite difficult to lead a family when parents are struggling to keep their own life in order.

Parents Have Poorly Formed Value Systems

Some parents fail to lead because they don't have a coherent, solid system of beliefs and values. A common example is the young couple who starts having children before they have a chance to develop a stable and mature sense of self. Their values and beliefs are still shifting from one year to the next or from one relationship, job, or neighborhood to the next. With a network of support and guidance, these young parents can continue to mature and learn important lessons while doing the job of being parents. But young parents can also be vulnerable to the negative influence of others and to disruptions that come from unexpected life stressors such as lost jobs, car wrecks, emergency room visits, and protracted health issues. A concerned neighbor, a sympathetic teacher, or a wise grandparent is often a pivotal resource for these parents. Importantly, being young, poor, or homeless or struggling with mental illness does not define a parent; nor does it dictate the level of love, care, and concern they provide for their children.

Parents' Values Are Prosocial but Dormant

Some parents, despite being hardworking and responsible, have children who are adrift on a valueless sea. This can happen when parents are private and silent about what matters most to them. Often, these parents prefer to let their actions speak for them. There are also parents whose families are busy with one activity after another, so messages about what is valued or important are lost in the shuffle. If you're a parent whose family is very active, consider using family structure to highlight and amplify your family's values and beliefs. For example, you could use routines and rituals to mark important occasions (e.g., birthdays) or to honor the people and things that are central to your family (e.g., graduations). These kinds of structures help parents slow down periodically and give voice to what matters most in life.

CONCLUSION

We've suggested that the task of leading is really one of "carrying." Parents who lead carry the water of serving the greater good of their family. They also carry messages with important life lessons and core family values and share them with their children. And finally, they carry themselves in a way that gives children a reason to follow their example. Leading emerges naturally from a parent–child relationship that combines acceptance with containment. And parents are better able to lead when they attend to their own health and well-being and take advantage of family structure and the Third Option.

LEAD HOMEWORK

- How do you serve your family? List the things you do that prioritize the needs of your family, even when it is unpleasant or inconvenient for you.
- Identify important but overlooked topics that deserve a conversation with your children (school and academics, drug or alcohol use, peers, dating and sex, money and career, identity).
- Practice using the Third Option ("I see you doing X. We believe Y.") and stopping at the period!
- To what extent are you a good example for your children? What are the areas of life where they benefit from watching and learning from you?

CHAPTER 8

NEXT STEPS: BUILDING YOUR OWN PARENTING PLAN

We began this book by noting that parenting can bring with it lots of emotions. Children give us moments of joy, pride, and love. But parenting can also bring difficult, unpleasant emotions as well as challenges, especially when children routinely express strong emotions and behave in difficult ways. Indeed, there are times when parenting means you love your child but might not like your child. Our aim was to offer a book that supports and guides parents, helping them be the parent their children need. It was not to make a pitch for perfect parenting, but to guide you toward good enough parenting. Our hope is that you become a parent whose capacity to accept, contain, and lead helps your children grow to be responsible adults.

We offered a holistic, long-term model of parenting that frames parenting as an effort to manage—over time—the relationship between you and your children. *It is this relationship that does much of the work of parenting.* It guides and supports children as they grow to become healthy, productive, and valued members of their community. Our holistic model runs counter to the notion that parenting is about controlling children's problem behavior in the short term. Building a solid, healthy parent–child relationship with a child who's prone to having strong emotions and difficult behavior requires a capacity to accept, contain, *and* lead. And parents' capacity to establish and maintain this kind of relationship for 18-plus years requires a foundation that combines (a) clarity about the goals of parenting, (b) emotional health and well-being, and (c) a structure to home and family that can bear the stress and strain of modern life. In this final chapter, we cover the next steps to building your own parenting plan. Our hope is that you take full advantage of what you've learned in the previous chapters and apply it to your own family. We'll walk you through the process of making your own parenting plan, but first let's meet two parents. We'll call them Desiree and Greg.

DESIREE: "I HAVE NO BUSINESS BEING A PARENT"

Desiree walked into the psychologist's office and announced that she was "really pissed" and didn't know what she might do next. She said she had "lost it" the day before, coming close to crossing the line between harsh parenting and outright abuse. When she had arrived home from a bad day at work, the house was a mess. She was exhausted but knew that coming home meant she had to cook dinner, supervise homework, and do laundry. She hoped her kids would have done their part to help but, on that day, no chores were done and no one had started homework. Desiree announced that she deserved better and complained, "No one gives a damn." The therapist didn't challenge Desiree or ask questions but gave her time to sort things out. Desiree started to cry, her shoulders sagged, and her chin fell to her chest. She stayed that way for a long time. After a minute or more, Desiree looked up and said, "I have no business being a parent."

Desiree is like many moms. She works, she's divorced, and she's parenting on her own. She's raising three kids and gets little or no help from other adults. In fact, other adults are often a source of stress when they judge her and her parenting. She feels that nobody understands or cares about her life's struggles. No one is around to witness the truly ugly moments of her parenting, times when she screams, threatens, and punishes way more than is necessary. Her parenting tirades have been more frequent in the past few months, and she feels that her life is falling apart, bit by bit. She doesn't know what to do.

The psychologist took time to honor all that Desiree was feeling—all the pain, frustration, and sadness weighing her down. In that moment, the psychologist wanted to respect Desiree's effort to be a better parent and to acknowledge her struggles as a divorced mother working full-time outside the home. There was no need to rush Desiree, to have her pull it together and make the unpleasant feelings go away. It was more important for her to know that there was at least one person in this world who understood what she was dealing with and had some idea of how crappy and confused she felt that day.

GREG: IN CHARGE, BUT NOT REALLY

Greg felt lost and didn't like it. Not one bit. He was a loving father, a successful businessman, and things usually worked out the way he planned. He had a keen, analytical mind and with just a bit of time there were few problems he couldn't solve. He was the picture of competence, but here he was in the psychologist's office feeling confused and incompetent. He had recently learned that his daughter, Sara, had been sneaking out of the house at night. She was apparently leaving to meet her boyfriend, but there were few other details. Greg wasn't sure he wanted the details. This was his "baby girl," and her behavior made no sense to him. He kept saying, "What is she thinking?!!" His anger was quickly starting to catch up with his confusion.

The psychologist suggested that any parent would feel upset if their 15-year-old daughter was slipping out of the house at night

215

unsupervised to be with a boyfriend. Greg appreciated the sympathy but didn't appreciate it when the psychologist suggested that Greg's confusion might be a good thing, an asset he could use as he tried to make sense of how to respond to Sara and her nighttime escapades. Some therapists are like that; they occasionally poke or prod clients who need help moving from an unworkable but all too familiar position to a new place that is scary but also growth promoting. Greg made a living telling others what to do; he didn't like crises or calamities, especially when they could have been avoided if folks followed his advice and did what was expected. So here he was meeting with a psychologist and faced with the fact that his daughter, Sara, had clearly ignored her father's expectations!

The psychologist knew that Greg's family was dealing with several issues and that Sara's recent behavior was just one part of the picture. Righting this family's ship was going to take a lot of work on their part. The psychologist's comment about Greg's confusion being an asset was an effort to slow him down, to fight his tendency to move quickly to bring folks back in line and put an end to his feeling frustrated, embarrassed, or worried. Greg's experience told him that if he acted quickly, he could regain control, as witnessed by his comments about imposing "martial law" at home until things were back on track. The psychologist, sensing an opportunity to help Greg make meaningful changes in the way he parented, asked Greg to say hello to confusion, to fear, and to frustration—his new allies on the journey to being a better father. Fortunately, Greg was curious enough to learn more.

This chapter aims to help you

- learn how to troubleshoot your current approach to parenting;
- see examples of how to apply a holistic, long-term model to parenting; and
- learn to build your own parenting plan.

TROUBLESHOOT YOUR CURRENT APPROACH TO PARENTING

Like Greg's therapist, we also encourage parents to use feelings of discomfort and doubt to improve their parenting. Although unpleasant, these experiences can signal when it's time to find your bearings and determine what, if anything, about your parenting needs adjusting. Figure 8.1 presents a troubleshooting guide with a recommended sequence for moving through key aspects of our holistic, long-term model of parenting. The underlying rationale in this troubleshooting sequence is working *outside-in.* That means focusing initially on areas outside the parent–child relationship. Before questioning your capacity to accept, contain, or lead, it helps to first consider other, more obvious issues—some of which are easier to fix. As we discussed in Chapter 1, many parents have the skills needed to build a good relationship with their children, but they often lack clear workable goals, adequate health, or sufficient structure for their home and family. Rather than assuming you lack the ability to build and maintain a healthy relationship with your children, it makes

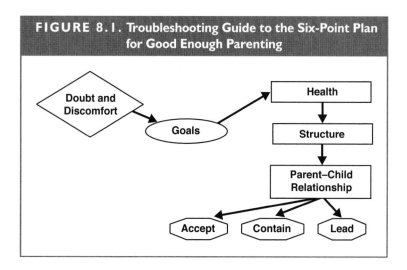

FIGURE 8.1. Troubleshooting Guide to the Six-Point Plan for Good Enough Parenting

more sense to consider first what might be interfering with those efforts. The parent–child relationship, like all relationships, can be adversely affected by several factors. We get busy, we get distracted, we grow tired, we feel stressed or overwhelmed, or we're unhealthy and don't get the help we need. When these occur, our capacity to accept, contain, and lead our children will suffer. Thus, the process of identifying which aspects of parenting need attention begins with goals, followed by a focus on parents' emotional health and their family's structure. Only after reviewing those aspects should parents consider whether they are providing the core conditions for a strong, healthy parent–child relationship.

Goals

Goals guide our behavior, but as we noted in Chapter 2, parents often lack goals specific to parenting. More common is for parents to have vague notions about what they're trying to do each day and distant dreams about their child's future. We also noted in Chapter 2 that much of parenting is done automatically without a lot of deliberate thought. When we're on autopilot, we can parent while also thinking about or doing other things. But that can be a problem when automatic, overlearned parenting is driven by goals that are hidden from our awareness and activated by various emotions such as anger and fear. Therefore, it can help to set clear, specific goals for how we want to interact with and parent our children. We drew from the science on risk and protective factors (see Chapter 2) to identify the kinds of goals that can guide parenting and promote healthy child development.

Let's say you're concerned about your 10-year-old son who is busting walls and bruising siblings (ages 5 and 14). If your chief parenting goal is to contain his aggressive behavior, then we—and the science of parenting and child development—would say that you're on the right track. If he was having other problems that often come with childhood aggression (e.g., poor grades, troublesome peers), then containing his aggression is without a doubt Priority One. If, on the other hand, your chief parenting goal is to help him get on a highly competitive basketball or soccer team, then an adjustment might be needed. Being part of a competitive sports team is not a bad goal, but it could be a goal that's more about impressing other parents or living your childhood dreams. It's certainly not the most important parenting goal at this time and will not necessarily promote your child's growth and development.

Health and Structure

Let's assume you decide to address your son's aggressive behavior, but he's uncooperative and you have doubts about how to go about it. What's more, your relationship with your 14-year-old daughter is also now starting to feel strained. A useful next stop in the troubleshooting guide (Figure 8.1) is to consider your own emotional health and the structure of your home and family. Recall that healthy parents have the energy, strength, and commitment needed to do the job of parenting. If you're worried about or are unsure about your own health, consider scheduling a visit with your primary care physician. We also recommend reviewing the health inventory presented in Chapter 3. This is the long list of things that we called health with a capital H, including emotional, physical, relational, recreational, and, for some, spiritual aspects of health. Evaluating your health status in these ways can help you know if you need to focus more attention on this aspect of parenting.

Perhaps you're feeling stressed by recent events or preoccupied with important tasks that lie ahead. Is your family moving soon, are you trying to sell your home, or you worried about finances because you're recently divorced? Moving your family to a different city or your children to a new school can be anxiety provoking. Are you exercising regularly or has that lapsed because of demands at work? If your job is stressful, do you have a plan for managing that stress and is it working? Have you been irritable, short-tempered, or impatient with your children? Do you feel tired and sluggish most of the time? These and other health-related issues can have a negative impact on your parenting. Perhaps it's time to combine your new parenting goal of containing your son's aggressive behavior with strategies that help you reclaim the energy, strength, and commitment needed to get back on track and do the job of parenting.

Structure

Let's say that your health was fine or that you have addressed health-related issues but were still concerned about whether you're adequately addressing issues involving your son and his older sister. The next place to look is the structure of your home and family. Staying with the same example, we can easily imagine how the upheaval of divorce, the stress of trying to sell your home, or the pressure to meet a work deadline can disrupt the way a family operates. And if your efforts to juggle all of this are affecting your health, then it makes sense to consider a shift in structure. Has your role as the parent and leader of the family changed of late? Has your family's routine been blown off course? Are there too many days where your children eat alone while you're at the computer or on the phone? Does your family need a standing rule about not hurting others or destroying others' things? Do you need to call a family meeting to check in with everyone and address these issues? Did you miss or mishandle an important major ritual (e.g., your daughter's birthday) or has your family stopped doing an important miniritual (e.g., weekly movie night)? All of these are distinct possibilities in this scenario and addressing them could be quite helpful.

The Parent–Child Relationship: Accept, Contain, and Lead

It should be apparent that factors "outside" the parent–child relationship (Goals, Health, and Structure) are critical to the job of parenting and problems in these areas could exist apart from how you interact with your children (Accept, Contain, and Lead). It's generally easier to tweak or recalibrate your parenting goals, and it's not terribly difficult to correct *temporary* dips in your health or to check the workability of your family's roles, routines, rules, and rituals. Indeed, restarting a valued family ritual or reminding your children about important household rules (e.g., "No hurting others") can seem like small steps, but they can have significant, positive ripple effects.

On the other hand, building or repairing a strong parent–child relationship can be a difficult task that won't happen overnight. This is more of a long-term project, but you can start *today* to establish a posture of acceptance. It might take several weeks before your children come to expect a consistent message of belonging, and it could take even longer before they see you as emotionally safe, available, and accepting. The same holds true for containing. For children to have a sense of containment, they must experience repeated occasions when you followed through on specific disciplinary targets. If they've witnessed times in the past when you reclaimed your disciplinary authority but soon faded from being "the Boss," they'll likely view your latest effort as just one more phase. If you're able to narrow your disciplinary focus to a few target behaviors that matter most (e.g., hurting others), there should be fewer occasions to demonstrate that you're willing and able to contain them, which means it could take even longer before they realize there's been a shift in your disciplinary focus. Finally, as we discussed in Chapter 7, your children will not see or respect you as a leader without a track record of combining accepting and containing.

One of the biggest challenges to improving or repairing a parent–child relationship is self-doubt and the temptation to question what you're doing. Depending on how harshly you judge yourself, you could get derailed. For example, if your benchmark for parenting (see Chapter 1) is whether your kids are happy and not complaining, how well they're behaving, or is it like how you were raised, you could be led astray. To make sure that doesn't happen, review earlier chapters and guidelines that speak to what it means to accept, contain, and lead.

APPLYING A HOLISTIC, LONG-TERM MODEL OF PARENTING: TWO EXAMPLES

We hope this book is a helpful resource that offers useful information and new insights you can apply to your own parenting, especially if your children are struggling emotionally and behaviorally. To help with that goal, we now return to the two fictional parents (Desiree and Greg) we introduced at the start of this chapter.

Desiree and Greg's stories represent—in our imagination— how parents might use this book and our holistic model of parenting to make needed adjustments. Recall that Desiree was a divorced mom trying to balance the demands of home and work. Greg was a married man with a successful business, but his teenage daughter was sneaking out at night. They're very different parents living in very different circumstances, but both stories illustrate how one might apply our holistic model to their own parenting.

Desiree: Back in the Business of Parenting

Desiree wasn't sure why her sister sent her this book, but she decided to read it anyway. She wanted to believe her sister just wanted her to know she was thinking of her, but Desiree feared the book was her sister's way of passing judgment on Desiree and her parenting. Of course, Desiree was doing a lot of that herself, questioning whether she should even be parenting. She loved her kids and they seemed to love her, but she felt like such a mess as a parent. She was always tired and cranky, and she couldn't get her kids to pitch in and do their part, which only made her more tired and crankier. She felt frustrated, lost, and hopeless. She feared that problems with her own health and well-being were getting in the way of her parenting.

When Desiree opened the book and read the vignette about the father and his son (Jason and Sean), she felt a bit of hope that this book would speak to her. She wasn't sure how parenting can be holistic or how it helps to know that it's a long-term job, but she saw herself in the section discussing different ways that parents judge their parenting. A few days later, she read about parenting Goals and child risk factors but wasn't clear what it meant for her and her kids. She agreed with the part about parenting often being mindless and automatic, driven by goals that are emotional and hidden.

She put the book down for a few days but later mentioned it to her sister when they talked by phone. In talking about the book, Desiree realized how much she had learned. So, she went back to the book and decided to read the chapter on Accepting, even though it wasn't next. She was intrigued by what she learned, realizing that wasn't how she was raised. The more she read, the more she wondered if her kids would ever see her as accepting. She decided to try some of the simple options for accepting and had fun parroting and paraphrasing what her children said to her. She saw how it pulled them to say more and more, even without her asking a bunch of questions. Excited by this, she read the chapter on Containing and a light bulb came on! Never had she heard that it's important to be *selective* in your discipline; she thought it only mattered if you were *effective* at discipline and being effective meant you followed through with what you said every time, which she had trouble doing. Desiree thought it made a lot of sense to focus only on a handful of behaviors and to be consistent with those few behaviors. That wasn't easy, though, because her kids were always into things and arguing with each other. She read and reread the section on time-out and response cost because she wanted to know effective ways to punish her kids if they needed it. She wasn't really a spanker, but she had done it a few times when she was mad, and her kids were a bit too old for time-out. She decided to use response cost as a sanction, and she came up with a short list of disciplinary targets.

Desiree wasn't sure how all of this was supposed to work, so she next read the chapter on Structure. Heaven knows her family needed more structure! She really, really liked this chapter. She especially liked the idea that she could organize her family by making a schedule, by having rules, and by creating little fun rituals. The part about roles hit home because she recognized that the generational boundary in their family was barely there. She was always dumping on them stuff she was worried about and did a horrible job protecting her own private time and space. She kept reading, focusing next on Health. This chapter helped her understand why she was struggling as a parent: She had zero energy and almost no strength. She realized that if she didn't do something about her health, that her commitment to the job of parenting would also be lost. She completed the health inventory and didn't like what she saw. She knew it was time to talk to somebody about her emotional health and that if she didn't take better care of herself, it would only hurt her kids. Desiree went to see her physician to talk about her feelings of depression. Her physician took time to learn about Desiree's troubles, discussed possible treatments, and recommended anti-depressant medication. Four weeks after she began taking the medication, Desiree realized she wasn't as cranky or as sluggish as she used to be. Her children were also in a better mood. They weren't taking medication, so it seemed that her feeling better, having more energy, creating better family structure, and narrowing her disciplinary focus were helping. When Desiree started reading the chapter on Leading, she became even more convinced that she was headed in the right direction. She started to see that she was doing a good job as their mom and that she was the leader of her family.

Greg: In Charge, Really

Greg's wife, Linda, saw the book and figured it couldn't hurt to buy it. Sara was a strong-willed girl—always was, always will be. Maybe there was something in the book that would help Greg. Linda had her own ideas about why Sara was sneaking out, but she didn't tell them to Greg. She read the first few chapters of the book and thought, "We're not doing too bad a job!" She mentioned it to Greg, letting him know how important it is that they continue to accept Sara while also being firm on a few important things, like not sneaking out of the house at night. Greg agreed and said he'd take care of it. Linda was hoping for a different response, perhaps the two of them working together to figure out what Sara needed. But once again, Linda thought this but didn't say it.

Linda was intrigued by the book's chapter on Leading and thought it made sense that their ability to be Accepting and Containing helped them with Leading their children. But she wondered about the family-wide aspect of leading: Who did the kids believe was leading their family? Despite Greg being the most vocal parent and a successful businessman, she wondered about the example he was setting for their children. She thought about that for a while, but again didn't say anything to Greg.

Greg excelled at most things and had high expectations for himself. He also liked a challenge and frequently took on one high-risk project after another. He was a good provider for his family, and they lived well. But 2 years ago, work had overwhelmed him. He was working on a project that presented financial risk and demanded a great deal of his time, although the potential payoff was huge. As it turned out, there was no way he could finish the project without sacrificing other aspects of his life. He decided to take the risk, believing the sacrifices were worth it. He couldn't walk away from the chance to hit a money-making home run. He told himself that he worked hard and was helping his family. Besides, if he didn't do the project, someone else would. In his mind, he could see his plan working out and believed that he was "so close" to pulling it off.

Unfortunately, Greg underestimated what it would cost him, his employees, and his family to take on the project. He channeled all his energy into work, hoping his wife and kids would hold it together until the stress of the project passed. But wives have expectations and kids have needs, and he had nothing more to give. "Not now!" was his mantra. He felt misunderstood and unappreciated. He shut down and pulled back emotionally from everyone. Well, almost everyone. "She" understood, only she wasn't his wife and her "understanding" included more than insight and advice. Repercussions from Greg's affair were big and immediate. In the end, the project was a bust, he lost the respect of his kids, and he nearly lost his marriage. He and Linda were able to reconcile after a brief separation and the family seemed back on track. But then his daughter, Sara, started sneaking out at night to visit her boyfriend. And Linda wondered what that meant about the state of her family.

Linda read the chapter on Structure and immediately recognized there was something missing in the way their family was organized. She couldn't put her finger on it, but she decided to talk with Greg about it. She read about boundaries, routines, and rituals and decided that she and Greg needed a ritual, a time when they could talk and be a team—a parenting team. Greg agreed to a regular date night, one where they would talk and be with each other and not with a dozen other people drinking and partying. Greg was very sociable, and a night out was almost a performance for him. Linda wanted his full attention. She showed him the book and said, "I've got some ideas, but first, I want you to read this book." Greg agreed, assuming there might be one or two things worth knowing from the book but otherwise it would be old news.

Greg was a quick reader, and he decided to start by reading about Accepting, Containing, and Leading. At their first date night, Linda asked what he thought so far. Greg said he thought they were already doing what the book recommended. Linda agreed but then asked,

> What about the part on Leading? What about the part that says it's good for leaders to serve others? And what about the Third Option, where you tell children what you believe but you don't do a lot of preaching. You just say it, you stop, and then you give them room to decide what to do?

She told Greg she didn't see him doing that with Sara. Greg felt hurt by Linda's questions and comments. They ended their date early.

Over the next few days, Greg read about Structure and Health and thought a lot about what Linda had said about leading. He asked himself: "Am I being a good leader to my family? Do I treat Linda as a coleader?" He read the chapter on Health and read parts about coping with stress. He thought about the ways he typically coped with stress. Clearly, he was someone who relied on problem-focused coping. He thought back to his affair and how it was a poor way to cope with the stress of work. He wondered if he needed to find other, better ways to cope. He decided to ask Linda about this during their date night. He was nervous but tried to tell himself he wasn't afraid to talk to his wife about coping, even though he rarely did it. Linda was surprised and wasn't sure what to say; she wasn't even sure what he was asking her. Did he really want to know what *she* thought about the way he coped with stress? Linda breathed deeply, feeling it in her gut and hoping to settle herself a bit before she spoke. She didn't want date night to go badly 2 weeks in a row. She told Greg she loved him but that he was not invincible. Yes, he was smart, caring, and thoughtful, but he had limits like everybody else. She said, "You need me, and you need your family, and your family needs you." She told him that if he was as smart as everybody thought he was, he'd spend more time working on his marriage and being a part of the family. She told him they weren't a team, that he didn't trust her when they had different ideas about the family or their kids. Yes, he could be "accepting" of his daughter, but it's not just about showing the world that you're accepting; sometimes it's about being quiet and still and just being with someone. She found herself saying, "Be with me, Greg! Be with me."

That night, Greg was up late. He was once again feeling lost and confused. Sara walked into the den and asked what he was doing. He said, "I don't know. I don't have any idea what I'm doing." Sara looked at him, puzzled. He saw it on her face, so he asked her to sit down. He told her that he was worried about her, worried about her sneaking out at night. He told her that he made mistakes, big mistakes, and there were times when he wasn't a very good example for his daughter:

> But I can tell you this, Sara. I'm done with sneaking out of this house. This is my home, and my family, and this is where I want to be. I hope it's where you want to be. Your mom and I are working to make our family and our home a place that you want to be. We want to be a family that you can love and be proud of. We haven't always done that.

BUILDING YOUR OWN PARENTING PLAN

This last section is one that you write, not us. It's where you put pen to paper (or fingers to keyboard) and build your own parenting plan. To aid in that process, we present a few writing exercises in Worksheet 8.1. The first exercises are designed to prompt reflection on what you've read and learned. The next exercises are more detail oriented, essentially working lists that cover the six domains in our holistic, long-term model of parenting. The last exercise asks you to identify your family's core values and to describe how your parenting will align with those values.

WORKSHEET 8.1. Reflective Writing Exercises

Goals

1. How would you describe what your current goals are as a parent?

_____

_____

_____

2. If you were to set a goal involving only one domain of our holistic, long-term model of parenting, which would it be and why?

_____

_____

_____

Health

3. Review the health inventory. Which aspects of your health are high points, and which are the low points?

_____

_____

_____

4. What are you doing currently to cope with stress, and how is it working?

_____

_____

_____

Structure

5. Grade your family (A through F) on how well your family is using each of the 4 Rs of structure: Routines, Roles, Rules, and Rituals.

_____

_____

_____

(continues)

WORKSHEET 8.1. Reflective Writing Exercises (*Continued*)

6. If you were to add or tweak one of the 4 Rs in your family, which would it be and why?

_____

_____

_____

Accept

7. Be honest: How long can you sit quietly with your child? Aside from your child thinking you're strange, what would be hard about doing that?

_____

_____

_____

8. If your children felt **completely safe with you and accepted by you**, what would be different about how you interacted with them? What would be different about how they interacted with you?

_____

_____

_____

Contain

9. Do you have a short list of specific target behaviors? If not, what would be on your list?

_____

_____

_____

10. Which sanctions are you likely to use and which are you not likely to use (and why)?

_____

_____

_____

WORKSHEET 8.1. Reflective Writing Exercises (*Continued*)

Lead

11. If you were a child, how likely would you be to follow the example of your current life and why?

_____

_____

_____

12. Do you believe your children respect you? If so, why?

_____

_____

_____

Your Parenting Plan

13. Please list what you consider to be your family's core values.

_____

_____

_____

14. Describe how your parenting plan aligns with those values.

_____

_____

_____

Reflective Exercises

DRAW YOUR FAMILY

Draw two pictures of your family. In one, create an organizational chart of your family. "Org charts" are used in business and government to show who's in charge, who answers to whom, and who's in the same department or division. Family therapists use a similar process to illustrate how families are organized: Who's in charge, who's aligned with whom, and who might be all alone. Therapists do this with input from families. Here's your chance to draw the org chart for your family. In the second drawing, show your family doing something it does routinely. It could be cooking, taking a walk, shopping, or going to church. Don't worry about how well you draw—just have fun with it. Once you're done with one or both drawings, take a moment to react. What do you feel and what do you think about what you drew? Is there anything new to be learned about how your family is organized or how your family interacts? If you're brave, show the drawings to your family and ask them for their reactions. This should be fun and educational!

Describe What It's Like Being in Your Home

Write two short "essays" (really, just a few words) that describe (a) what it's like *for you* being in your home and (b) what it would be like for a *nonfamily member* to hang out in your home. The first question is a way to ask how your home is structured, so consider the 4 Rs (Routines, Roles, Rules, and Rituals; see Chapter 4) when you describe being in your home. The second question is one we often ask families. The goal is to get a sense—at a visceral or gut level—of what it's like to be in your home. Would a guest feel relaxed and comfortable or tense and ready to leave? Is yours a home where family members could suddenly erupt into an argument or does your home feel relaxed and welcoming?

Working Lists

These exercises are designed to help you review the six domains from our holistic, long-term model of parenting, with the goal of taking stock of what's going well and what might need adjusting. This is the kind of exercise that can be done with your coparent if you have one. That way, you can work as a team to build your own parenting plan. Another option is to do this with another parent who has their own family. In fact, imagine doing this exercise with your book group of five or six other parents. Oh, the conversations you could have!

A FINAL NOTE FROM LAUREN AND TIM

From Lauren

I have dedicated my life to studying and serving families to improve their parent–child relationships. This usually means working with one family at a time. So, when Tim asked me to join him on this book and potentially reach many families all at once, I jumped at the opportunity. I've had the joy and privilege of seeing families go from being argumentative and stressed to being communicative and supportive. Hopefully, this book can do that for other families. When I think about the defiant, demanding, loud toddlers I've met in my work, I'm amazed at how big they seem—as if their tiny bodies suddenly grew to take up the entire room. But once parents learn how to accept, contain, and lead, they walk into that same room and their children seem small, adorable, and loving—like an entirely different child. Truthfully, I feel incredibly lucky to be trusted to help and to be a resource for parents and for your family. My hope is that this book allows you a front-row seat to the magical process of your family's positive transformation.

From Tim

Like Lauren, I feel privileged to work with and support parents on the important job of raising their children. Our writing this book and you reading it are not the same as meeting you in person and getting to know you and your family. It's not the kind of relationship we have with the families we see in our practice. But it has certainly felt like a relationship to us, writing this book with you in mind. We have tried to do right by you, to be respectful, and to serve you well. When we were stuck or unsure, we'd think of those parents who are working hard to do right by their children even when no one saw it. So, thank you for the time you've taken to read this book. We hope it was time well spent.

REFERENCES

American Sleep Association. (n.d.). Sleep hygiene tips. https://www.sleep-association.org/about-sleep/sleep-hygiene-tips/

Cavell, T. A. (2001). Updating our approach to parent training. I: The case against targeting noncompliance. *Clinical Psychology: Science and Practice, 8*(3), 299–318. https://doi.org/10.1093/clipsy.8.3.299

Cavell, T. A., & Quetsch, L. B. (2023). *Working with parents of aggressive children: Process and practice* (2nd ed.). American Psychological Association.

Chödrön, P. (1991). *The wisdom of no escape: And the path of loving-kindness.* Shambhala Publications.

Covey, S. R. (1991). *The seven habits of highly effective people.* Covey Leadership Center.

Darwin, C. (1895/2004). *On the origin of species.* Routledge.

Greene, R. W. (2010). Collaborative problem solving. In R. C. Murrihy, A. D. Kidman, & T. H. Ollendick (Eds.), *Clinical handbook of assessing and treating conduct problems in youth* (pp. 193–220). Springer Science + Business Media. https://doi.org/10.1007/978-1-4419-6297-3_8

Kabat-Zinn, J., & Kabat-Zinn, M. (2021). Mindful parenting: Perspectives on the heart of the matter. *Mindfulness, 12*(2), 266–268. https://doi.org/10.1007/s12671-020-01564-7

Kushner, H. S. (2007). *When bad things happen to good people.* Anchor.

León-del-Barco, B., Mendo-Lázaro, S., Polo-Del-Río, M. I., Fajardo-Bullón, F., & López-Ramos, V. M. (2022). A protective factor for emotional and behavioral problems in children: The parental humor. *Children (Basel, Switzerland), 9*(3), 404. https://doi.org/10.3390/children9030404

McKee, L. G., Parent, J., Zachary, C. R., & Forehand, R. (2018). Mindful parenting and emotion socialization practices: Concurrent and longitudinal associations. *Family Process, 57*(3), 752–766. https://doi.org/10.1111/famp.12329

National Institute on Alcohol Abuse and Alcoholism. (1997). *Special report to the US Congress on alcohol and health from the Secretary of Health and Human Services* (Vol. 9).

National Institute of Mental Health. (2022). *Health topics.* https://www.nimh.nih.gov/health/topics

Orrell-Valente, J. K., Hill, L. G., Brechwald, W. A., Dodge, K. A., Pettit, G. S., & Bates, J. E. (2007). "Just three more bites": An observational analysis of parents' socialization of children's eating at mealtime. *Appetite, 48*(1), 37–45. https://doi.org/10.1016/j.appet.2006.06.006

Patterson, G. R., & Yoerger, K. (2002). A developmental model for early- and late-onset delinquency. In J. B. Reid, G. R. Patterson, & J. Snyder (Eds.), *Antisocial behavior in children and adolescents: A developmental analysis and model for intervention* (pp. 147–172). American Psychological Association. https://doi.org/10.1037/10468-007

Rutter, M. (1989). Isle of Wight revisited: Twenty-five years of child psychiatric epidemiology. *Journal of the American Academy of Child & Adolescent Psychiatry, 28*(5), 633–653. https://doi.org/10.1097/00004583-198909000-00001

Shapiro, S., Siegel, R., & Neff, K. D. (2018). Paradoxes of mindfulness. *Mindfulness, 9*, 1693–1701. https://doi.org/10.1007/s12671-018-0957-5

Shapiro, S. L., & Carlson, L. E. (2009). *The art and science of mindfulness: Integrating mindfulness into psychology and the helping professions.* American Psychological Association. https://doi.org/10.1037/11885-000

Sheeran, P., Aarts, H., Custers, R., Rivis, A., Webb, T. L., & Cooke, R. (2005). The goal-dependent automaticity of drinking habits. *British Journal of Social Psychology, 44*(1), 47–63. https://doi.org/10.1348/014466604X23446

Wolin, S. J., Bennett, L. A., & Jacobs, J. S. (1988). Assessing family rituals in alcoholic families. In E. Imber-Black, J. Roberts, & R. A. Whiting (Eds.), *Rituals in families and family therapy* (pp. 230–256). Norton.

Zolotor, A. J., Theodore, A. D., Chang, J. J., Berkoff, M. C., & Runyan, D. K. (2008). Speak softly—and forget the stick: Corporal punishment and child physical abuse. *American Journal of Preventive Medicine, 35*(4), 364–369. https://doi.org/10.1016/j.amepre.2008.06.031

INDEX

Disciplinary Funnel in, 154–164
effective discipline for, 148, 150–151
fixed-ratio system for, 151–154
four-step approach to, 172–188
homework for, 189
instructing in, 173–174
as key element of parent–child
relationship, 24
in leading, 191, 197–198
in parenting plan, 221–222, 228–233
reconnecting in, 185–186
sanctioning in, 175–185
seeing results of, 87
selective discipline for, 148–150
useful options for, 186–188
warning in, 174–175
Contexts of children's lives
competing, 89
in good enough parenting, 87
managing, 17–19, 89
nonparent relationships, 20–23
parent–child relationship, 19–20
Control, over children's behavior, 5–6
Coping
consequences of forms of, 38–39
self-care portfolio for, 78–79
strategies and preferences for, 75–78
Correcting work, 185
Covey, Stephen, 59–60

Darwin, Charles, 61
Day care, 21
Decisions, that benefit whole family, 193
Delinquent acts, 162–164
Describing what you see, to convey
belonging/acceptance, 125
Dictator-type parents, 23
Dinner
getting together at, 109
trying to get children to eat more
at, 133
Disciplinary Funnel, 154–164
disciplinary targets in, 154–157
using, 157–164

Disciplinary script, 171
Discipline. *See also* Contain/containing
consistent, 166–169
effective, 148, 150–151
nonviolent, 171, 177–185
physical, 176–177
reconnecting after, 185–186
selective, 148–150
"Divide and conquer" situations, 96
Divorce, power struggles in, 94
Do and Don't rules, 159–160
Downstream effects of parenting, 10
Drinking
and family dinners, 109
socializing and, 33
speaking openly about, 196

Effective discipline, 148, 150–151
Effective parenting, myth of, 7–8
Efficient parenting, structure for, 88
Efforts of parents, outcomes of parenting
vs., 16–17
Emotional health. *See also* Emotions
and avoiding emotions, 67–69
and eating dinner together, 109
of parents, 39, 47, 51, 218, 219
and problems in parenting, 56–57
Emotional management, 67–69, 134
Emotional rewards of parenting, 5
Emotion-focused coping, 76, 77
Emotion regulation, with parental
posture of acceptance, 139–142
Emotions, 56–79
acting on, and not feeling, 63–64
being open to, 59, 60
of children, evaluating parenting
based on, 13–15
of children, trying to make sense
of, 125
of children, tuning in to, 14–15
coping strategies and preferences,
75–78
defined, 57
facts about, 57–58

ABOUT THE AUTHORS

Timothy A. Cavell, PhD, is a professor in the Department of Psychological Science at the University of Arkansas and a practicing clinical psychologist. In his academic role, he trains doctoral students to be therapists and studies how parents, teachers, and mentors can help and support children facing various challenges (e.g., aggressive behavior, school bullying). He and his wife have three children.

Lauren B. Quetsch, PhD, is a professor in the Department of Psychological Science at the University of Arkansas. She obtained her BA in psychology from Georgetown University and her PhD in clinical psychology with a specialization in child clinical psychology at West Virginia University in Morgantown. Dr. Quetsch's expertise is in children with disruptive behavior disorders and adapting evidence-based treatments for children on the autism spectrum. She also prioritizes the dissemination and implementation of evidence-based treatments for underserved families in community mental health organizations. She and her husband have four wonderful children.